MW01121334

THE
ELECTRONIC
★ ★ ★ ★ ★ ★ ★
BATTLEFIELD

Bob Guerra

COMPUTE! Publications,Inc.**abc**

A Capital Cities/ABC, Inc. Company
Greensboro, North Carolina

ISBN 0-87455-117-X

COMPUTE! Publications, Inc., Post Office Box 5406, Greensboro, NC 27403, (919) 275-9809, is a Capital Cities/ABC, Inc. company and is not associated with any manufacturer of personal computers.

Contents

Section 4. Future Battles

Part 3. Geopolitical Decision Making

Appendices

Foreword

The Electronic Battlefield is the perfect resource for any electronic war gamer. Detailed descriptions of 30 of the most popular computer war games show you how they work, how to play them, and how to win.

Computers are tailor-made for war game play. Their number-crunching abilities, memory, and speed make them fierce opponents and impartial referees. Millions of people play war games, and more of them are turning to computerized versions for their entertainment. Board games are old hat to this new generation of gamers. Electronic battlefields are in.

This book takes advantage of this trend toward computer games, and offers general and specific hints, tips on play, and winning techniques for each war game. The book is partitioned into sections on joystick-oriented games ("At the Front"), strategic and tactical simulations ("In the War Room"), and world-wide political and military conflicts ("Geopolitical Decisions"). Within each section, games are grouped by type (land, sea, or air battles) so that the reader can easily locate the game he or she is looking for.

Some of the games included in *The Electronic Battlefield* are best-selling classics such as *F-15 Strike Eagle*, *Arctic Fox*, and *Lords of Conquest*. Newer games, destined to sell big in the genre, can also be found in *The Electronic Battlefield*—games like *Balance of Power*, *Up Periscope!*, and *Destroyer*.

Written by a dedicated war gamer who has spent countless hours battling electronic foes, *The Electronic Battlefield* will appeal to players of all ages and levels of experience. The author reveals undocumented features of many of the games, and has pored over manuals and historical accounts. He's provided winning strategies for every game, so that even a beginner has a chance of beating computerized generals and admirals.

Such a thorough reference wouldn't be complete without command reference charts, maps, and other illustrations to help players play better. And a comprehensive appendix lists all the information readers need in order to buy the 30 games included in *The Electronic Battlefield*, as well as many other popular war games.

Bob Guerra has made *The Electronic Battlefield* an indispensable guide every gamer will want.

★ PART 1 ★

ON THE FRONT
(Joystick Battles)

★ SECTION 1 ★
NAVAL BATTLES

1
PHM Pegasus

Ships flying across water? It's possible, as hydrofoils attest. And as you'll see in PHM Pegasus, *it's an exciting sight. Guns blazing, missiles firing, and chaff flying, pit yourself against all comers in this out-of-the-ordinary naval action game.*

★★ Scenario 8: Jihad ★★

It happened first with the U.S bombing of Lybia in 1986. A scenario originally written for a computer simulation—*F-15 Strike Eagle*—was played out for real in the Middle East. Then, again in May 1987, history seemed to imitate a computer war game when an Iraqi jet fighter attacked the U.S.S. *Stark* with Exocet missiles, prompting the United States to consider escorting Kuwaiti oil tankers through the Persian Gulf.

This is the description of the Jihad scenario from Electronic Arts's *PHM Pegasus*, a game released several *months* before the attack on the *Stark*:

> *Your mission is to escort a supply ship out of the Persian Gulf. The only complication: A war is going on, and innocent ships are being fired upon without warning. . . You will need to make your way through the Straits of Hormuz to Kuwait where you will rendezvous with the supply ship.*

Now it doesn't take any real genius, or even a crystal ball, to figure out that continued U.S. and Soviet military presence in the Middle East is likely to lead to confrontation, if not with the two superpowers, then with the countries already at war. The foreshadowing of world events in computer war games shows that many designers are considering not only the military hardware, but also the world affairs that could lead to the use of those weapons.

Although the Pegasus-class hydrofoil may never really see any action in the Middle East, *PHM Pegasus'* Jihad scenario is a good example of the kind of missions the PHM hydrofoil might be suited to. Some of the other missions that you can undertake include intercepting and sinking terrorists' patrol vessels in the Mediterranean, before they can return to their base on Cyprus; photographing cargo ships suspected of smuggling arms to a dictator; and escorting a medical supply ship to a group of refugees in South America.

The scenario you select will determine the type of hydrofoil you will command—the *PHM Pegasus*, the Israeli *Flagstaff II*, or the Italian *Sparviero*. All three hydrofoils use identical instrumentation and are capable of the same speed and maneuverability. The only difference among the three ships is the type of missile each carries.

Weaponry

The three types of game missiles are the Harpoon, the French-made Exocet (the type used against the *Stark*), and the Gabriel. Both Harpoons and Exocets can be used against enemy ships up to 40 miles away, and they will find their targets nine times out of ten. One hit from either missile can destroy a small patrol vessel, but it may take two or more hits to eliminate larger attack crafts and missile corvettes.

Gabriels don't have quite the range of the Harpoons and Exocets, but they do have a greater accuracy and a high-explosive 400-pound warhead. Because of the guidance systems built into all three types of missiles, they don't have to be aimed at their selected targets.

Since you usually carry only eight missiles out to sea, they shouldn't be wasted on targets you can handle with the hydrofoil's 76mm Oto-Melara cannon. This is the weapon of choice for any small enemy ships within ten miles of your boat. Try to close to within six miles of any moving target, however; targets between six and ten miles away, though technically within your cannon's range, can't be targeted with any real accuracy. No matter which scenario you select, you'll begin with 400 rounds and can fire at a rate of 90 rounds per minute. The Oto-Melara is water-cooled to prevent overheating.

The hydrofoil is also equipped with 20–24 chaff rockets that can be launched as decoys to confuse enemy radar-guided missiles. While it's not absolutely necessary for you to select a specific enemy missile as your target before you fire the chaff, it's a good idea. Targeting a missile makes it more visible on the radar screen, which makes it easier to evade. (And to tell when it's a mile away—the optimum time to let a chaff rocket fly.)

Instrumentation

Of course, a powerful weapons system won't do you much good without a sophisticated radar system to guide you in its use. At the maximum setting, the round radar display in the center of the Pegasus instrument panel shows you all ships and aircraft within a 40-mile radius. The viewing radius can be changed to display 20 miles, 10 miles, 5 miles, or 2.5 miles. At each setting, your hydrofoil is shown as a blinking dot in the center with the area in front of your ship shown at the top of the display.

Before you can select an enemy ship as a target, it must appear on the radar screen. Once selected, the ship is shown through the binocular view at the top of the screen. When attempting to hit an enemy ship with your 76mm cannon, you should use the aiming cursor and aim-corrector light to guide your shots. Although the rapid-fire cannon allows you to fire several rounds with a single squeeze of the joystick button, you'll conserve ammunition and improve your accuracy by pausing between shots to make adjustments according to the aim corrector light. Figure 1-1 shows what the instrument panel looks like.

Since both your missiles and chaff rockets are also fired with the firebutton on your joystick, you must choose the current weapon for firing. A weapons indicator at the left of the *Pegasus* control panel shows the selected weapon, as well as the

Figure 1-1. Instrumentation Screen

number of rounds, rockets, and missiles remaining. In addition to the radar display, the center of the panel also has gauges showing the amount of fuel you have left, your hydrofoil's speed in knots, and your engine setting. A gyrocompass is included, and indicators on each side of the radar display warn you when enemy missiles have locked onto your ship, or whether you are entering shallow water.

The right side of the instrument panel contains your hydrofoil's damage indicator. This graphic display shows the degree of damage to your engines, fuel tank, radar system, missiles, chaff launchers, and 76mm cannon. In addition, damage to any of your six hull compartments is shown here. Any system or hull compartment may suffer light damage (shown in yellow) or heavy damage (shown in red). Usually, minor damage causes a system to work less effectively, while heavy damage completely disables it. For example, minor damage to your missiles can cause them occasionally to misfire, while heavy damage to your missiles make them totally inoperative. Heavy damage to four of the *Pegasus'* hull compartments will cause it to sink. The *Flagstaff II* will go down with heavy damage to just three compartments, while the smaller *Sparviero* sinks after heavy damage to only two hull compartments.

The Big Picture

The instrument panel and binocular view are fine when you're busy battling it out on the high seas. When there aren't any enemies within range of your radar, however, or when you must navigate long distances, you should use the operations map. This is accessed from the bridge screen by pressing V on your keyboard.

The operations map shows the sea and surrounding land areas as well as the positions of your ship and any auxiliary crafts, such as helicopters or convoy ships, that you control. The radar radius of each friendly vessel is displayed as a circle around the vessel, and any enemy ships that fall within that radius are revealed. By spreading out your radar-equipped vessels so that their radar circles almost meet, you can scan a large part of the seas.

Figure 1-2. *PHM Pegasus* Scenario Map

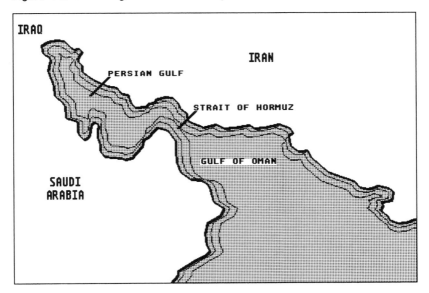

A one-point course can be set for any of your vessels by selecting the vessel, choosing one of five engine settings, moving the cursor to the desired destination, and pressing the firebutton. However, since this allows you to plot only a straight-line course, ships must be guided around land masses by using a series of short courses. Helicopters, on the other hand, may reach any destination by using a single one-point course regardless of land masses.

The speed of the currently selected vessel, the elapsed time since the start of the mission, and the total time you're allowed to complete the mission are displayed beneath the operations map. By pressing the plus (+) key, you can compress time to 128 times normal. The time scale, in effect, is also shown in the operations map (Figure 1-2).

Strategy and Tactics

At the beginning of the Jihad scenario, your Pegasus-class hydrofoil and both auxiliary helicopters are positioned several miles to the southeast of the Strait of Hormuz in the Gulf of Oman. The supply ship that you must escort out of the Persian Gulf is sitting off the coast of Kuwait. Although you may be tempted to begin moving the supply ship southward to meet your hydrofoil halfway, any movement by the convoy ship without your hydrofoil by its side for protection will invite an attack by the Iranians. You must first sail all the way to Kuwait before even thinking about moving the supply ship.

To determine whether there are any potentially hostile vessels between your hydrofoil and the Strait of Hormuz, send helicopter 1 to the middle of the strait, and send helicopter 2 to a point midway between your hydrofoil and helicopter 1. This will give you radar coverage of almost the entire course to the Strait of Hormuz, and will allow you to avoid most of the OSA I and OSA II missile corvettes that are patrolling in the Gulf of Oman. While it may take a little extra maneuvering to avoid a confrontation, getting to the strait safely is more important than getting there quickly.

Play It Safe

If necessary, sneak up to the strait along the coast, well away from any enemy activity. Set your hydrofoil's speed to maximum, and increase the time scale to at least 64 times normal. Otherwise, the trip to the Strait of Hormuz could take all day. When your hydrofoil reaches the radar circle of helicopter 1, plot a new course for helicopter 2 that takes it into the Persian

Gulf, midway between helicopter 1 and the small peninsula (Qatar) that juts into the gulf from East Arabia. This will let you see what's waiting for your hydrofoil on the other side of the strait.

If, as you maneuver your hydrofoil toward and through the strait, it appears from the operations map that you're coming close to any enemy ships, lower your engine setting, reduce the time scale with one or two presses of the minus (−) key, and return to the bridge. Identify the blips that appear on the radar by cycling through them with the target-selection key. Once you have figured out which, if any, of the blips represent enemy ships, you can take over control of the hydrofoil and manually steer away. Then, return to the operations map and reactivate the automatic course that you previously have established.

Change Course

Making your way through the strait will require several minor adjustments to your course, and the time scale should be set to no greater than 32 times normal as you snake your way through. As you leave helicopter 1's radar circle and move into helicopter 2's scanning range, you should set your speed back to maximum, crank up the time scale, and decide on the best course, or combination of short courses, to get you safely to Kuwait. Just be sure to leapfrog helicopter 1 past helicopter 2's radar circle, once again, to give you radar coverage at the northern end of the Gulf.

Although, ideally, you'd like to reach the supply ship without having to defend your hydrofoil against attack, this isn't always possible. If you hear the splash of enemy shells hitting the water near your ship, return immediately to the bridge and try to steer your way out of trouble. If the enemy ships in the gulf won't let you carry out your mission peacefully, you'll just have to Harpoon them.

Under Attack

If you come under attack, go to the bridge and select the closest target that's in front of your ship. If all of the enemy ships are behind your hydrofoil, use your greater maneuverability to swing around to face them. Then, select the closest target and launch a Harpoon missile. Immediately select another target and launch a second missile. If there are more than two attackers, you'll have to chase down the third and eliminate it by using your deck gun.

In your haste to rid the area of hostile ships, don't neglect to protect your own ship from any missiles that might be headed your way. Rather than simply firing off two or three chaff rockets as soon as the warning indicator goes off, however, you should wait until the missiles are within a mile of your ship. Careful timing will make your chaff system more efficient.

When you finally reach the supply ship, set parallel, but not identical, courses for both your hydrofoil and the supply ship. Because the supply ship's maximum speed is only 26 knots, you'll have to set the speed of your hydrofoil to only 30 knots to keep the two ships close together. While the ships must remain close together, a collision at sea could abruptly end the mission without the enemy having to fire a shot. Therefore, whenever there is no immediate threat, put a small amount of distance between the ships while keeping both ships as far as possible away from any other ships that may be traveling through the Gulf.

As you did on the trip north, leapfrog your two helicopters to provide constant radar coverage of the areas your ships travel through. The key to a successful mission is patience. If you try to rush into and out of the gulf in one mad dash, you're bound to lose either the supply ship or your own hydrofoil. Take your time and plan each phase of the mission carefully, and you could get promoted to admiral.

2
Up Periscope!

Submarine simulations can't reproduce the cramped quarters, boredom, and terror of World War II undersea warfare. What they can do is put you behind the periscope and in command of your own fleet class submarine. That, Up Periscope! *does—and does well.*

Until Spectrum Holobyte released *Gato* in 1983, no one had ever created a realistic graphic simulation that put the player in the control tower of a submarine. Since then, at least three companies—Microprose, ActionSoft, and Epyx—have all climbed aboard the underwater bandwagon. The resulting simulations—*Silent Service, Up Periscope!,* and *Sub Battle*—all do a great job of capturing the danger, excitement, and occasionally, the tedium of submarine warfare. But of all the software subs, *Up Periscope!* offers the best blend of realism and playability.

One reason is the game's cleverly designed display. While *Silent Service* makes you run between three separate screens to check your instruments and gauges, maps, and periscope view, *Up Periscope!* puts everything you need on a single screen.

Screen Information
As you patrol the enemy-controlled waters of the South Pacific, the bottom third of the screen displays your main instruments and gauges. Thus, valuable information on the status of your weapons, propulsion, and navigation systems is always visible. The top portion of the screen shows the bridge/periscope view. It can be split so that maps, radar, or the sub's Torpedo Data Computer (TDC) are simultaneously displayed on the right. In addition, a single status line at the top of the

screen lists each function key and highlights those that have been selected.

Other displays that are accessed less often—such as the patrol and damage reports, and larger maps of the entire patrol area—are loaded from disk as needed; they cover the entire screen. The four available patrol maps are the North Pacific Theater, the South Pacific Theater, Hawaii, and the training area at New London, Connecticut.

Instrumentation

At the left of the instrument and gauges display is a torpedo status indicator that shows which of the forward and aft tubes are loaded. A digital readout shows how many additional torpedoes are held in reserve. Unlike some submarine simulations in which a single key is used to empty the next available tube, *Up Periscope!* requires you to select your tubes by number. Therefore, as a scenario progresses and tubes are emptied and refilled, it's important to check this display to determine which number keys correspond to the currently loaded tubes.

The fuel levels section of the display uses horizontal bars to show the diesel fuel, battery, and oxygen levels. Usually, if you're playing one of the shorter "Historical Situation" scenarios as opposed to a full-fledged patrol, you'll have to consider only your battery and oxygen supplies since you'll begin with more than enough diesel fuel to complete the scenario. In fact, unless you must travel submerged at top speed for long periods, your battery and oxygen levels will require little monitoring. Figure 2-1 shows the instrument panel.

Below the fuel level section you'll see the water temperature, the current time scale being used (you can accelerate the flow of time up to 32 times normal), the time, day of the week, and date. If you could strap your computer and monitor to your wrist, you'd have a watch.

In the center of the instruments display is a rotary compass with a digital course readout and a rudder position display. This information is critical to any successful attack because, often, the only way to find the enemy is by matching your course to the enemy's bearing, as displayed on the TDC.

Figure 2-1. *Up Periscope!* Screen

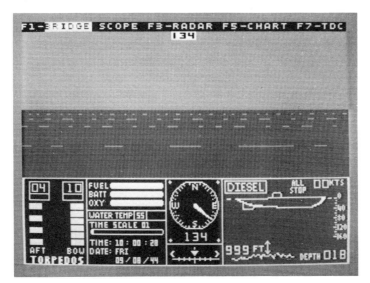

The final section of the display is the master status indicator. In all, eight important facets of the sub's operation are shown here, including the engine setting, speed in knots, whether diesel fuel or battery power is being used, the sub's depth below the water's surface, and the remaining depth below the keel. Unless you're patrolling close to shore, however, you won't have to worry about running aground.

Weapons

The Fleet-class submarine from which you command is equipped with the standard configuration of six forward and four aft torpedo tubes. These are all full when you begin your patrol, and 14 additional torpedoes (10 in the bow and 4 aft) are held in reserve. One feature of *Up Periscope!* that adds to the simulation's playability, while slightly detracting from its realism, is that whether you select a bow or an aft tube, the torpedo will always take a straight course according to the periscope bearing. Therefore, once you've emptied all 6 forward tubes, you don't have to swing the sub around before using your aft torpedoes.

The type of torpedo you carry depends on the time period of the historical situation selected. Early in the war, the Mark 10 torpedo was used. It was a lot slower than newer models, but more reliable. The torpedo that saw the most action during the Second World War was the Mark 14 steam torpedo. Though faster than the Mark 10, the Mark 14 had a faulty detonator that resulted in a high percentage of duds. An electric torpedo—the Mark 18—was finally introduced early in 1944, and for the first time, the United States had a reliable torpedo. Although the USS *Rasher* patrol, described below, took place in September 1944, the Mark 14 is used as the default torpedo. Whether or not this was the torpedo actually used on that patrol is not clear, but it seems to do the job.

TDC

No matter which torpedo your sub is armed with, you should always use the TDC to lock in your targets before firing. Like *Silent Service, Up Periscope!* lets you set the TDC on either automatic—enabling you simply to point and fire—or manual. In both simulations, the manual TDC requires player input before locking in the target. The main difference between the two systems is the type of input needed. *Silent Service* requires that you enter an estimated angle-on-the-bow, while *Up Periscope!* requires only that you take at least two marks at about a minute apart.

Marks are entered simply by pressing the M key when the periscope is aligned with the enemy's bearing. Once a mark has been entered, the TDC begins tracking the target and displays its bearing, course, speed, range, tonnage, and ship type. The target's range is determined with radar, sonar, or a split-image optical system called a *stadimeter*. Each system has its limitations. For instance, radar range-finding can only be used during surface attacks and, therefore, should be used almost exclusively at night. Sonar, unfortunately, is easily detected by the enemy because it works by emitting an audible signal. Finally, because the stadimeter is an optical system, it is effective only when there's good visibility.

Although the torpedo is the fleet submarine's primary weapon, your boat is also armed with a small deck gun. This weapon may have been useful for skeet shooting when the patrols got boring, but it certainly had little use in battle. While it can be used to hit targets out to about 1700 yards, it's nearly impossible for you to damage an enemy ship by using only the deck gun. In fact, on one patrol, I hit a tanker at least a dozen times using the deck gun without even slowing the ship.

Tactics
★★ Historical Situation 7 ★★
USS *Rasher*, Fifth War Patrol, August 18, 1944

Before beginning this scenario, you may want to stop at the Features menu to adjust the default date. Although this patrol took place on August 18, 1944, the default date for the scenario has been mistakenly programmed as August 18, *1950*. While this will have no effect on the outcome of the patrol, sticklers for historical accuracy will surely want to make the adjustment.

When the game starts, call up the patrol map, zoom in to setting number 4, and you'll see six ships to the southeast of your sub at a bearing of about 140 degrees. This is a three-ship convoy consisting of a 9750-ton tanker, a 3900-ton transport, and a 3750-ton freighter, escorted by three 1500-ton destroyers. Call up the TDC and switch from stadimeter to radar range-finding. Then, take a mark. The computer will begin tracking a 1500-ton destroyer moving at 12 knots on a 205-degree course. Since the destroyer is over 14,000 yards away at this point, you won't be able to spot it visually, but if you keep your binoculars trained to the bearing of the destroyer as shown on the TDC, you'll always have it in your gunsights.

To intercept the convoy, you should change your course to 180 degrees so that you are heading directly southward. Then, turn your binoculars back to the bearing of the enemy and increase your speed to 20 knots by setting the engine to Ahead Flank. Since the attack will take place at night, there's no need to approach the convoy submerged.

Alternate occasionally between the small patrol map and TDC displays to get an accurate fix on the enemy's position. Take additional marks every couple of minutes to improve the accuracy of your torpedoes when it comes time to fire. When you close to within 6000 yards, cut back to Ahead Full. The submarine will slow to 12 knots (matching the destroyer's speed), but you'll still be gaining about four yards per second on the destroyer because your courses intersect.

One Down

As you get closer, the destroyer's bearing will begin to increase more rapidly. Be sure to keep the destroyer in your sights. At the same time, try to maintain a bearing with your binoculars that's about two to three degrees greater than the destroyer's bearing shown on the TDC. When the bearing of the binoculars reaches 180 degrees (the destroyer's bearing will be 177–178 degrees), stop panning the binoculars, take a final mark, and wait for the enemy to cruise directly into your line of fire. Ideally, you should be within 4000 yards.

As soon as the destroyer's bearing reads 180 degrees, fire the torpedo from tube 1. Then aim two degrees to the left (178) and unload tube 2. Finally, turn your sights back to the right to 182 degrees and empty tube 3 to complete the spread. Once the third torpedo has been fired, cut your engines back to about one-third ahead and be ready to take evasive action if any of the convoy's destroyer escorts decides to give chase.

Often, at least two of the three torpedoes will find their mark, and the first of three destroyers will be on its way down. Check the patrol map to confirm that there are now only five ships to the south of your submarine. Then, just for fun, check the patrol report, and you'll see that the sinking of a 1500-ton Japanese destroyer has already been logged.

Although a bearing of 180 degrees was used in this attack, there's no reason that you can't fire on the enemy ship before its bearing reaches 180 degrees. In fact, because the enemy is on a 205-degree course, any bearing between 115 and 180 degrees will give you a reasonably broad target. As the bearing edges up past the 180-degree mark, however, you'll begin facing the stern of the enemy ship. Therefore, you'll have considerably less target to aim for. No matter what the enemy's exact bearing, make sure that you close to within 4000 yards before firing, and then, launch a spread of three torpedoes. The first should be aimed directly at the bearing indicated on the TDC, and the others should be fired 2 degrees on either side.

Two to Go

When you return to the bridge after sinking the first destroyer, call up the TDC once again and reset it. Otherwise, it will continue to track the estimated position of the sunken destroyer. Take a mark and, with any luck, the TDC will pick up and begin tracking one of the two remaining destroyers assigned to escort the convoy. The target should still be close to 7500 yards away, since it's assigned to cover the opposite side of the convoy.

Now that the convoy has passed to the south and you're no longer in a good firing position, you must alter your course to run almost parallel, but more westerly, than the enemy. If your boat hasn't been detected, the convoy should still be maintaining a 205-degree course. Adjust your course to about 235 degrees and increase your speed to Flank once again. This should get you ahead of the convoy as you move westward.

When you've increased the distance between youself and the enemy destroyer to around 8000 yards, turn back toward the south. This will put you in about the same relative position as in the first attack. Eliminate the second destroyer by firing tubes 4, 5, and 6.

In for the Kill

With two of the three destroyers sunk, you can now go after the tanker, freighter, or transport with less chance of reprisal. After each attack, be sure to go to the patrol map—it's the best way to determine whether any remaining destroyers have discovered your position and are about to come gunning for you. If this happens, don't panic. It's night, so simply increase your engine setting to Ahead Flank, swing the boat around, and head to the northeast. If you get a good head start, the cover of the night will let you quietly slip away.

3
Silent Service

In this simulation of World War II submarine warfare in the Pacific, your main weapon is the torpedo. Since you can't return to base for a fresh supply of torpedoes when you run out, every launch must count.

During the Second World War, the submarine emerged as one of the United States' most important naval weapons. Despite problems with torpedo design that persisted throughout most of the war, U.S. subs in the Pacific enjoyed great success against Japanese warships. And, perhaps more important, they were able to cripple the Japanese war effort by mining shipping lanes and sinking over 5 million tons of tankers and cargo ships. In addition, U.S. submarines served a vital reconnaissance role, providing important information on the movement of Japanese fleets.

On the surface, the U.S. Fleet Submarine used four 64-hundred-horsepower diesel engines to slice through the water at a maximum speed of 20 knots. Underwater, the sub could travel at only half that speed, and then for only short periods, using battery-powered motors. With the boat at a depth of 44 feet or less, a captain could spot enemy convoys using the periscope, and then sneak up to launch a surprise submerged attack. If detected by Japanese destroyer escorts, the sub could dive to as much as 425 feet, leaving the enemy with no real target except the sub's last known position. If the sub remained near the surface too long, however, a carefully placed depth charge by a fast-moving destroyer could send the captain and crew to a watery grave.

Man the Torpedoes

In *Silent Service,* as in real submarine warfare, your main weapons are torpedoes launched from tubes at both ends of the submarine. Altogether, there are ten tubes—six forward and four aft—and you begin patrol with all of them loaded. Fourteen additional torpedoes are available (8 fore, 6 aft) but it takes about ten game minutes to reload an empty tube. And since you can't return to base for a fresh supply of torpedoes when you run out, you have to make every launch count.

According to the specs, your Mark 14 steam torpedoes have a maximum range of around 4500 yards—you'll find that it's hard to hit the broad side of a burning tanker at that range. This is especially true when you're playing at a historical reality level where the torpedo's course is unreliable over long distances. In most cases, you'll want to close to within a couple thousand yards of the target ship (preferably approaching it broadside) before firing.

If you're playing one of the early scenarios, such as the Growler Patrol discussed later in this chapter, you'll want to head for the cover of the deep as soon as you've launched torpedoes. Otherwise, Japanese escorts will be able to trace the Mark 14's bubble stream right back to your sub. The electric Mark 18 wakeless torpedoes, which are available in later scenarios, make it easier for you to remain hidden longer, but they don't provide you with an immediate visual confirmation that your shots are closing in on the target. It's hard to know whether to fire more torpedoes at the same angle, or, if you're entering your own angle-on-the-bow estimates into the Torpedo Data Computer (TDC), whether to add or subtract several degrees.

Torpedo Data Computer

If you don't enter your own angle-on-the-bow estimates because you're confused by the explanation in your *Tactical Operations Manual,* here's how it works.

With the angle on its default setting, 0, the torpedoes will always fire straight out of the front or back of the sub. Thus, as long as your periscope bearing *matches* your heading (or is

180 degrees different), your torpedoes will launch at whatever's lined up in the crosshairs. In this situation, you can lead a target moving to the right by entering a positive angle-on-the-bow estimate (usually 10–25 degrees, depending on the target's range and speed), or, if it's moving to the left, by entering a negative number of degrees.

If your bearing and heading don't match, then the angle-on-the-bow will be the number of degrees difference, plus the number of degrees (10–25) that you want to lead the target. For example, if your heading is 25 degrees, and you spot a destroyer with your periscope bearing 80 degrees, you'd start with 55 degrees (80 − 25) as the angle-on-the-bow. Simply add another 10–25 degrees if the destroyer is moving to the right, or subtract that amount if it's moving to the left. Remember, a bearing of 5 degrees and a heading of 355 means an angle-on-the-bow of −10, not 350.

The Torpedo/Gun Practice option provides an excellent setting to test your angle-on-the-bow estimating ability. If you still have a hard time hitting the targets, you should either pass up this reality option or keep your periscope bearing aligned with your heading as much of the time as possible.

No matter how you aim your torpedoes, it's often a good idea to fire three or four at a time, using the angle-on-the-bow to separate them by five to ten degrees. This way, you're bound to hit something if there are several ships within range and they're clustered together. Just remember, you can launch a maximum of four torpedoes at any one time; subsequent launches simply replace the lead torpedo.

Deck Action

Your submarine is also equipped with a 4-inch deck gun that can be used for surface attacks. While the deck gun isn't particularly powerful, and it often takes several direct hits to sink anything, there are a number of situations where you'll have to use it. You might be out of torpedoes; your torpedo tubes may be damaged or in the process of being reloaded; or you may have to defend your sub against destroyer attacks, if damage to your diving planes makes submerging impossible. Also, since your torpedoes' warheads aren't even armed until they've traveled at least 450 yards, the deck gun is your only defense when a ship comes within this range. If an enemy vessel gets this close, however, you should quickly put some distance between you and the charging ship, before your sub is rammed. Even cargo ships may try this tactic if you get close enough; it's often more dangerous than a direct hit from a destroyer's gun.

The deck gun always fires in the same direction as your periscope bearing (regardless of the sub's heading) and can be used against targets as much as 8000 yards away. The gun's firing range is automatically set by the TDC, but you can adjust the gun's deflection manually.

To calculate the deflection, check the target ship's speed and range on the TDC display to determine whether it's moving toward or away from your sub, and at what speed. If possible, bring the sub to a stop to obtain a range reading that's based solely on the enemy's movement. Estimate the distance (in yards) the target will move in the time it takes a shell to reach it. Remember that the closer the target, the faster your shells will arrive, and the less time the ship will have to move from its original position. Finally, enter the number of yards you expect the target to move either toward ($-$) or away ($+$) from you.

Since you head out to sea with 80 shells, don't be afraid to use them. Immediately after the first shot, fire another—this time 25 yards closer—and a third, 25 yards farther away. Note the one that finds its mark, and pound away using that setting. If all three miss, double-check your calculations and try again.

Gauging Your Progress

Whether you're in the conning tower looking through the periscope, up on the bridge searching for the enemy through binoculars, or down below charting your course on the patrol navigation map, most vital information concerning the sub's status is onscreen at all times. This includes your speed, heading, depth, whether you're diving or surfacing, and your throttle setting. In addition, messages pop up at various times to warn you of such things as low battery level, empty or damaged torpedo tubes, test depth being exceeded, and approaching destroyers.

The Instruments and Gauges battle station also displays most of this information, but its real use is to give data that isn't available anywhere else. For instance, unless you keep a mental note of the number of fore and aft torpedoes you've fired, you should check the instruments and gauges screen to see how many torpedoes you've got left. The number of remaining deck gun shells is also displayed. See Figure 3-1.

Figure 3-1. Instruments and Gauges Screen

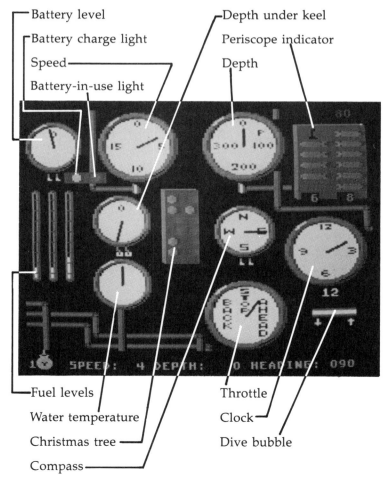

Another useful bit of information found on the instrument and gauges screen is the time of day. Since dusk and dawn are great times to launch attacks on enemy ships (you can use the periscope but they have a hard time spotting you), you might want to check the clock occasionally to help time your strikes.

When battling it out near land, the depth under the keel can be more important than depth below the surface. There's nothing worse than chasing a convoy of cargo ships for hours, only to beach your submarine because they've tricked you into following them too closely to shore.

Finally, the water temperature gauge can be important in helping you escape from enemy escorts. When the dial turns blue, it means you've passed below a strong thermal layer— the enemy's sonar will have a harder time finding you. Most of the time, however, you should dive as deep as safely possible, regardless of the thermal gradient layers.

★★ War Patrol ★★
USS *Growler*, August 1942, Brisbane

To play a challenging scenario that can provide an excellent rating without being frustrating, select the Commander skill level and choose the Limited Visibility, Convoy Zig-Zags, Port Repairs Only, Convoy Search, and Angle-on-the-Bow Input reality levels. The other two reality options, Expert Destroyers and Dud Torpedoes, are only for players who can graciously accept being sunk without even scratching the enemy, or who don't mind finally getting a torpedo to hit a zig-zagging destroyer that's closing in, only to have the torpedo go *splash* instead of *bang*.

When playing the *Growler* patrol, there are a couple of things to keep in mind. First, since it's August 1942, you'll be using the older Mark 14 torpedoes. Though their bubble stream does make it easier for enemy destroyers to track you down, their speed (16 knots faster than the newer Mark 18) can be a real advantage. Second, the improved pressure hull that allowed U.S. subs to dive to 425 feet is still a year away, so you'll only be able to safely dive to 300 feet. Figure 3-2 is a map of the *Growler*'s second patrol.

Figure 3-2. USS *Growler*'s Second Patrol

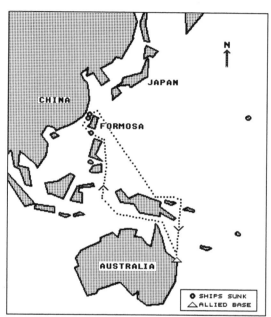

The Hunt

As the patrol begins, you find yourself off the coast of Australia, several miles to the east of your base in Brisbane. Since the *Silent Service* war patrol scenarios don't require you to intercept a specific convoy, or cruise to a particular trouble area, you're free to explore any part of the patrol map. Although the centerfold map of the Pacific, in your *Tactical Operations Manual*, shows the primary Japanese convoy routes reaching only as far south as Java before curving to the northeast through the Makassar Strait to the Palau Islands, there's actually plenty of action right off the coast of New Guinea. By heading north toward New Britain, the large island between New Guinea and the Solomons, you should be able to sight the enemy within a few days.

Spot and Chase

The first thing to do after a report of a sighting, is to go to the conning tower or bridge and try to spot the enemy by rotating the periscope or binoculars 360 degrees. When you see the enemy ships on the horizon, take note of the bearing and turn the sub until you're heading in that direction. Readjust your periscope bearing to match your heading. Surface, set the throttle on Flank Speed Ahead, and increase the time scale. As soon as the enemy ships begin taking shape, set the time scale back to normal and try to identify the ships as soon as possible.

Sometimes you'll be lucky enough to find a small convoy of unescorted cargo ships that you can simply chase down and blast out of the water. If the convoy is escorted by a single destroyer, you might try to eliminate it first.

Down the Throat

Follow the convoy until you're spotted by the destroyer and it starts to come after you. When this happens, dive to 44 feet (during daylight), cut the throttle back to one third, and use your periscope to watch the charging destroyer. If you're patrolling at night, remain on the surface and watch the destroyer from the bridge, using binoculars.

When the destroyer gets to within 2500 yards, quickly fire a spread of three or four torpedoes in its direction, and dive as you use full left or right rudder to cut away. Increase the throttle back to flank speed and continue to run from the destroyer, straightening your rudder when you're heading directly away from the pursuing escort. When it comes to within 500 yards of your sub, shut off the engines and continue diving until you reach a depth of 300 feet. Then, just sit and wait.

If none of your torpedoes hit the oncoming destroyer, it'll soon pass overhead and may drop a depth charge or two. It's likely, however, they'll be set to detonate long before they reach you. The destroyer might circle around a couple of times but should eventually give up on you and head back to join the convoy. When it does, quietly surface and try engaging the destroyer once again. If you win this little game of cat-and-mouse, you'll be rewarded with an unprotected convoy. Just don't use up all of your torpedoes on the destroyer, or you'll be stuck shelling the cargo ships with your deck gun and may only be able to sink one or two.

Patience

Unfortunately, most of the time the convoys you encounter will be accompanied by two or three very protective escorts. It's unrealistic to think that you'll be able to eliminate all of them and still have anything left to throw at the convoy. In cases like this, you have two options. You can either continue your patrol in another area, or try an end-around attack to pick off as many of the cargo, tanker, or troop ships as possible before the destroyers can close in and give you and your crew an indoor pool.

When you're planning such an ambitious attack, there are several things to keep in mind. First, submarine warfare takes a lot of time. You start with almost two months worth of fuel, so don't hesitate to swing very wide of the convoy to head them off at the pass, even if it takes all day. Also, remember that dusk and dawn attacks can be more effective than attacking in broad daylight or in the middle of the night. Finally, when you're up against a major force, such as three destroyers, don't be greedy. Spend a lot of time setting up for a few good shots, and then submerge and hide for a while.

If you get into trouble and the mission starts looking like a rerun of *Voyage to the Bottom of the Sea*, don't forget your emergency procedures. If enemy destroyers are closing in on your damaged sub and you fear another depth charge could end the mission, release fake debris to trick the destroyers into thinking you've sunk. Blow the emergency tank to reverse an otherwise uncontrollable dive, and be prepared to fight it out on the surface using your deck gun. Finally, if you manage to evade the enemy, but don't think you're in any shape to continue the patrol, just try to make it back to Brisbane. After a little shore leave, you'll be ready to slip quietly back into the deep.

4
Destroyer

Your mission as commander of a WWII escort destroyer is to see that a merchant convoy safely reaches its destination. All around are enemy subs and planes just waiting to attack. Will you make it through?

★★ Scenario ★★
Convoy Escort; Level: Intermediate

Because of her speed and fire power, the Fletcher-class destroyer is often considered the most versatile of all the warships. This reputation was earned during World War II when the destroyer proved useful for a variety of missions. These included patrolling for enemy submarines, supporting U.S. Marine invasions in the Pacific, escorting merchant convoys, and protecting Allied task forces from air attacks.

At full throttle, the Fletcher could cruise to trouble spots or pursue enemy subs at a top speed of 36 knots. If you've played *Silent Service*, you know what it's like to try to evade a destroyer that's quickly closing in on your submarine. With *Destroyer*, you get to experience this same type of exciting cat-and-mouse action. This time, however, it's *your* responsibility to protect a slow-moving merchant convoy from enemy subs, and see that it safely reaches its destination. In this simulation, submarines are just one weapon the enemy uses to get to your convoy. As captain of the destroyer, you'll also have to protect the cargo ships from enemy planes and warships.

Missions

Convoy Escort is just one of seven available missions. Others are Subhunter, Screen, Scout, Bombardment, Blockade Runner, and Rescue. Each scenario and level will challenge you with a different combination of threats. In the Subhunter scenario, for example, you'll simply have to search the patrol area for one, two, or three enemy subs (depending on the difficulty level) and eliminate them by using your depth charges. The Blockade Runner mission, on the other hand, requires you to reach a besieged island outpost, despite opposition from six ships, two submarines, six island gun-emplacements, and two dozen enemy planes. To reach your objective in this scenario, you'll need to use virtually every weapon and sensing station on board. Table 4-1 lists the enemy forces you can expect to face on every mission and level.

Table 4-1. Opposition at All Scenarios and Levels

Threat Level	Ships			Subs			Planes			Gun Emplacements		
	Eas	Int	Adv	Eas	Int	Adv	Eas	Int	Adv	Eas	Int	Adv
Sub Hunter	0	0	0	1	2	3	0	0	0	0	0	0
Screen	0	0	0	0	0	0	16	56	96	0	0	0
Scout	1	2	4	1	2	3	16	32	48	2	4	6
Bombardment	1	0	0	0	1	2	10	18	24	1	3	4
Blockade Runner	2	4	6	0	0	2	0	12	24	2	4	6
Convoy Escort	1	2	0	0	1	5	16	32	4	0	0	0
Rescue	0	1	2	0	1	2	0	16	24	0	3	5

Taking Charge

Destroyer is played at a number of battle stations; at which station or stations you spend most of your time depends on your objective and the enemy you're facing. To move from station to station, you enter the appropriate two-letter code: RA for Radar, DC for Depth Charge, and so on. The complete list of codes can be found in Table 4-2.

Of all the stations, the bridge is the most important, although you won't necessarily spend most of your time there. When you play difficult scenarios where you're up against multiple threats from planes, ships, and submarines, you'll spend most of your time jumping back and forth among your weapons stations. Nevertheless, the bridge is the brain of your ship. By flipping the right switches here, you can interact with just about every other station.

Table 4-2. Keyboard Control Codes

Function	Keys
Bridge	BR
Navigation	NA
Observation Deck	OB
Radar	RA
Sonar	SO
Guns Forward/Guns Aft	GF/GA
Antiaircraft Guns Port/Antiaircraft Guns Starboard	AP/AS
Torpedoes Port/Torpedoes Starboard	TP/TS
Depth Charges	DC
Damage Control	DA
Targeting Radar	TR
Abandon Ship	AB

For example, by using the top row of switches, you can call up reports from your radar, sonar, and damage control stations (Figure 4-1). Although important messages concerning enemy movement and damage also appear on the central message display found on every station screen, this section of the bridge lets you double check for any messages you may have missed.

Figure 4-1. The Bridge Screen

31

At the Helm

Below the report section on the bridge screen, are the helm controls. These allow you to either pilot the ship manually, when you feel like taking the wheel, or flip on the automatic pilot, so the ship will follow a course you've previously plotted on the navigation screen. Other options let you automatically run an evasive course, so the enemy will have a harder time hitting you (it's actually much safer to steer your own way out of danger), or automatically pursue an enemy sub while you're busy tossing depth charges over the side. No matter which helm mode you select, however, it's important to remember that you have to set the throttle yourself.

Captain Sharpshooter

The bottom two rows of switches are used to communicate with the crews that man the four weapons systems. When you select GQ (General Quarters) or Condition 1, all weapons stations will aim and fire automatically. Condition 3 lets you turn off all weapons systems at once. Condition 2 is activated when you use the bottom row to control the weapons systems individually.

Although you are the captain of your destroyer and shouldn't have to protect your vessel singlehandedly, the sad truth is that your crew isn't exactly a team of sharpshooters. In fact, if you rely on the crew to keep the enemy at bay, you may be in for a short mission. Whenever concurrent attacks by more than one type of enemy force (planes *and* ships, for instance) require that more than one defense system be used at the same time, always take the antiaircraft guns yourself. The crew has a tough time hitting anything that moves very fast and should be left to handle the main guns, torpedoes, or depth charges. As soon as you've downed the last enemy dive bomber, however, you should relieve the crew at one of the other battle stations.

Steering, Seeing, and Navigating

Below the one-line message display, is the helm. This lets you steer the ship and set the throttle on full, half, slow, stop, or slow reverse. In addition, your current heading and speed, in knots, are displayed here. The helm is duplicated on the radar and sonar screens, as well as on the observation deck.

The observation deck is similar to the periscope/bridge screen of *Silent Service* in that it lets you scan the horizon in a 360-degree sweep around your ship. This is about the best way to spot enemy ships before they're close enough to fire at you.

You may plot a course consisting of from one to four points through your patrol area. This is done at the navigation screen using a joystick-controlled cursor to set your coordinates. If the helm is already set on automatic, the course will begin as soon as you've entered the final point, and the ship will proceed under the slow throttle setting. If the helm is set on manual, or if you want to increase the ship's speed, you should go to the bridge or observation deck after plotting the course to activate the automatic pilot and adjust the throttle.

Proper use of the navigation screen can be more important than many players realize. Of all the ways that a mission can end unsuccessfully, three of them can be directly attributed to mistakes made in navigating your ship. The first way to lose through poor navigation is by having your ship leave the patrol map. Although warnings will be printed on the message display when you approach the edge of the patrol area, it's easy to overlook them when your eyes are searching the sky for approaching planes.

The second way poor navigation can cost you your ship is if you sail too close to an island's shoreline and run aground on the coral reefs. Be careful, when plotting your courses, that you don't cut corners too sharply when trying to circumnavigate an island.

The third way your course can spell disaster, is if you don't leave enough distance between your destroyer and the convoy of cargo ships you're supposed to be protecting. Since your ship simply stops when it has reached the final point in a preset course, be sure to get it moving again in a hurry if the convoy is closing in from the rear. Those cargo ships will run into you if you inadvertently park in their shipping lane.

You may want to stop by the radar or sonar screens occasionally, if things are a little slow. Since advance warning of enemy subs, ships, and planes appears on the message display, regardless of your present station, these screens can usually be safely overlooked.

Damage Control

Aside from the weapons stations, the final station you should become familiar with, before setting sail, is damage control. Damage to 10 of your destroyer's 13 stations will sink your ship, so it's important to use your four repair crews—Alpha, Baker, Charlie, and Delta—effectively.

Although damage is repaired automatically, how fast the repairs are made depends on the crew assigned to that area. Since Alpha is the fastest, you'll want to use it to repair damage that directly affects your ability to defend the ship or sail out of danger. In other words, use Alpha to repair anti aircraft guns when under air attack, or the destroyer's engines when both have been damaged and you're being shelled by enemy ships or island gun-placements. If you're not in imminent danger of sinking from damage, don't waste time with damage control. These crews are really all quite competent and, left on their own, will get you out of most jams.

Battle Stations!

Your destroyer is equipped with four weapons systems—5-inch main guns (fore and aft), torpedoes, antiaircraft guns (port and starboard), and depth charges. You're provided with an unlimited supply of ammunition for every weapon, except your torpedos. Fortunately, with *Destroyer*, the strength of your other weapons systems makes your torpedoes much less important than they were in real naval warfare during World War II. In fact, despite the torpedo's reputation as the destroyer's sting, all seven missions can be successfully completed without your ever emptying a tube.

Main Guns

These powerful weapons are effective against island gun-emplacements and can usually sink enemy ships with a single hit. When you arrive at the forward or aft gun stations, activate the targeting radar by entering TR, and then select the blip on the radar screen, at which you want to aim. Simply match the point and train settings calculated by the targeting

radar, and fire away. When you shoot at island gun-emplacements, if the first few shots don't result in "Direct Hit" messages from your crew, use the radar to recalculate the proper
settings.

Antiaircraft Guns

This is my favorite battle station. Maybe it's the way the enemy dive bombers spin off into the water under a trail of black
smoke when you blast them out of the sky. There really isn't
much strategy involved here. Just line them up in your sights
and pull the trigger. Aside from practicing, however, there are
a few things you can do to improve your chances of successfully fending off an entire squadron.

First, as soon as you arrive at one AA Station (starboard,
for example), always type the code of the other (port), but
don't hit the Return key. If the enemy planes manage to
knock out the gun you're using, you can quickly switch to the
other just by hitting Return.

Second, always return your gunsight to the center of the
screen when there are no planes visible so that you don't get
caught on the wrong side.

Third, fire only when you've actually got a plane lined
up, to avoid overheating your gun. Finally, since they've already done their damage, don't aim for planes flying away
from your destroyer if it will cause you to miss those that are
coming toward you.

Depth Charges

As soon as an enemy sub is reported patrolling in your area,
go to the bridge, select the Pursue helm control, and set the
throttle on Full Ahead. Then, go to the depth charge station
and use the first of your K-guns to launch one off the side
with a depth setting of only 15 feet. Then, roll a second one
off the stern rack with a depth setting of 100 feet, and a third
off the other stern rack, set at 200 feet. As you continue to
drop depth charges at various depth settings, pay attention to
the messages that appear on the display. These will tell you
whether the last depth charge that exploded was too shallow
or deep, or whether the sub was completely out of range. If

you're much too shallow or too deep, you're off by at least 100 feet. Otherwise, adjust the setting by about 50 feet, and you should be right on target.

Torpedoes

As previously mentioned, you destroyer's torpedoes aren't all they're cracked up to be. If you find that an enemy ship is closing in, but isn't within range of your main guns, you may want to take a shot with your port or starboard torpedoes. Just remember to lead the enemy vessel and fire two or three torpedoes at a time, if you think there's a good chance of hitting it. Otherwise, this is one weapon you can leave to the crew. They can't do any harm with the torpedoes, and they may make the lucky shot that gets you out of a dangerous situation.

Tactics

Now that you know nearly everything there is to know with regard to running a tight ship and keeping her afloat in the hostile waters of the Pacific, there are only a few tactical matters to discuss before you volunteer for Convoy Escort duty.

The most important thing to remember when you're escorting a valuable convoy of cargo ships, is never to leave the convoy in order to chase some ship or submarine, unless it's the only remaining threat. Without your protection, the convoy can easily come under attack; you may not be able to return in time to save it.

As the mission begins, you find your destroyer about 5000 yards north of the four-ship convoy. At the navigation screen, plot a one-point course that will take you about 15,000 yards directly northeast of your starting position. Then, go to the observation deck, flip on automatic steering, set the throttle on Slow Ahead, and do a 360-degree visual sweep for enemy ships. Often, you'll spot one or both of the scenario's two enemy ships directly to the northeast; you can go to your forward gun, line up with the targeting radar, and sink the threatening vessel with a couple of shots. Make it quick, though, because before long, the first squadron will arrive to keep you occupied while the enemy's sub slips silently and unseen into position to begin picking off the convoy ships.

When you receive word over the message display that an enemy sub has been spotted, go to the bridge and activate the depth charge crew. While you're at it, you might as well wake up the torpedo crews, especially if there's still an enemy ship around. For the remainder of the mission, keep alternating between the navigation and observation deck screens, responding personally to air attacks, and closely monitoring your proximity to the convoy so that you remain within about 5000 to 10,000 yards to the north. Remember, the mission can still be successfully completed, even if one of the cargo ships is sunk. Lose half the convoy, however, and the mission comes to an abrupt end.

★ SECTION 2 ★
AIR BATTLES

5
Jet

Jet gives you the thrill of flying both F-16 Fighting Falcon and F-18 Hornet jet fighters in a fast-moving, three-dimensional simulation. The hard part comes when it's time to land.

Landing a modern combat jet like the F-18 Hornet on the deck of an aircraft carrier has to be one of the most nerve-racking routines any navy flyer is required to do. To the pilot soaring through the clouds at 5000 feet, the carrier must seem like a cork bobbing in a vast tub of water. To the guys on the flight deck with the lighted batons, protective headphones, and fluorescent orange vests, each approaching jet must bring back visions of World War II film footage of crippled Wildcats skimming the deck before sliding uncontrollably into the water or, worse, into the carrier's superstructure.

If you've ever played *Jet* by Sublogic, you know that landing your F-18 on the carrier's deck after a successful dogfight or target strike is often the most difficult part of the mission. However, the satisfaction of finally catching that trip wire and safely jolting to an abrupt stop makes up for all of the watery crash landings and disastrous near misses. Of course, you could play it a little safer and fly all of your missions in the land-based F-16, but since *Jet* is the only jet combat simulator available that actually allows you to land back on the carrier (*F-15 Strike Eagle* requires only that you buzz the carrier at a low altitude), this chapter will deal with both the dogfighting and target-strike missions as flown in the F-18.

Instrumentation

Whether you fly the carrier-based F-18 Hornet or the land-based F-16 Fighting Falcon, the control system and instrumentation are the same. In either case, increase and decrease the throttle with plus (+) and minus (−) keys, respectively. Control the aircraft's pitch and bank angle with the joystick or keyboard.

With either plane, the onscreen cockpit, though not particularly realistic, presents important flight data in a logical format that's easy to read. For example, vertical gauges along the left and right sides of the cockpit window provide you with a graphic readout of the jet's altitude and speed. The aircraft's heading is displayed at the top center of the window, and most of the other instruments, including a small radar screen, are displayed along the bottom.

This bottom section of the display includes gauges showing the amount of fuel you have remaining and the current throttle setting, as well as indicators to tell you the status of your landing gear, speed brake, and afterburners. In addition, the magnification factor is displayed here (you can zoom in up to eight times normal), as well as which of the available weapons is currently armed. Also, a circular range indicator appears in the center of the Heads-Up Display (HUD) and can be toggled on and off. This indicator turns black when the enemy is within range of the currently selected weapon. Finally, a pitch indicator can be superimposed over the HUD to show you the approximate number of degrees your jet is pitched above or below the horizon. Most of the time, this indicator is just a needless distraction and should be left off. However, if you become disoriented during a steep climb because your window has suddenly become full of sky, the pitch indicator can help you get your bearings. Figure 5-1 shows the instrument panel.

Figure 5-1. *Jet* Instrument Panel

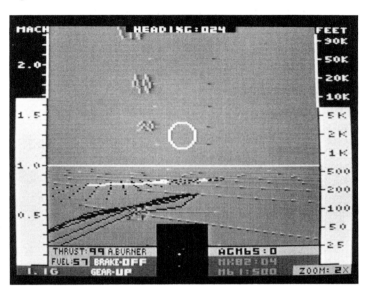

Weapons

After you've selected the jet and your mission, proceed to the arming menu. Here, depending on the scenario selected, you'll have a choice of air-to-air missiles, air-to-ground missiles, and bombs. For a dogfighting mission, you may choose from one to six AIM-9 Sidewinders or AIM-7 Sparrows. Since the Sparrow is a medium-range missile effective to a range of 25 miles (compared to just 5 miles for the short-range Sidewinder), you should take all six. After all, you want to be able to hit any enemy MiGs before their missiles can home in on you.

Of course, to compensate for the additional weight (each Sparrow weighs in at 500 pounds), you should take only two Sidewinders. Although this will still make your plane 680 pounds heavier than if you had selected the default setting of four Sidewinders and four Sparrows, the added weight won't significantly affect your plane's maneuverability. Besides, you'll lose 500 pounds as soon as you launch your first Sparrow.

In the target-strike mission, you can choose from one to six AGM-65 Mavericks or MK-82 bombs. The Maverick is an optically guided missile that's accurate from about 14 miles. However, the missile's small warhead requires that it be right on target to do any damage. The MK-82, on the other hand, is a *gravity* weapon; it simply falls to earth once it's released. That means you practically have to fly directly over the target before releasing it. With SAM units of one type or another guarding every ground target, this can be pretty dangerous. The 500-pound MK-82 has such a large warhead, however, that even a near miss will usually get the job done.

Take six of the longer-range AGM-65s, and only two MK-82s as backups.

One weapon you'll have on every mission is your M-61 20mm cannon. While this won't do you any good on a target-strike mission, it can be used at close range against enemy MiGs during the dogfighting sequences. At takeoff, this weapon is loaded with 500 rounds of ammunition. Each squeeze of the trigger fires 20 rounds.

The most important thing to remember about your M-61 is that you should avoid getting close enough to the enemy to use it.

Dogfighting

Before the modern combat jet was developed, aerial dogfighting meant pushing your plane to the limit to get a positional advantage—usually behind and slightly above your enemy. Then, the perfection of various air-combat maneuvers, such as the *yoyo*, *Immelman*, and *split S*, could often mean the difference between a successful mission and getting blown out of the sky. Today, long-range missiles and on-board computers are making this type of high-altitude heroics a thing of the past. When everything works according to plan, a pilot in a modern jet fighter like the F-18 can pick up an enemy fighter on radar, launch a medium-range missile such as the Sparrow from several miles away, and destroy the enemy plane without ever actually seeing it.

When playing *Jet*'s scenario, you should adopt this long-range approach to dogfighting and never let the enemy MiGs become more than just a blinking dot in the sky.

Up, Up, and Away

If you've read the *Jet* operating manual, you know that taking off from the deck of the aircraft carrier is a fairly simple procedure. You increase the throttle until the afterburners ignite, and press L to launch from the catapult. As your aircraft is literally hurled down the deck, your speed will gradually increase. When it reaches Mach .5, you'll become airborne and your altimeter will read 100 feet. Wait until this occurs before pulling back on the joystick. If the plane fails to respond appropriately and you repeatedly end up in the drink, the program may be failing to read your joystick and you may have to reboot.

Once you've cleared the deck, push your nose down slightly but continue to climb as you simultaneously bank to the right. Since you take off at a heading of 90 degrees and the enemy MiGs are usually to the south, banking right will allow you to face your targets quickly. As your heading nears the 180-degree mark, you should be able to spot two MiGs through the cockpit window. The plane on the left should be blinking, indicating that this is the currently selected target.

At this point you must pull out of the turn so the MiGs are centered, raise your landing gear, and toggle on both your radar and range indicator. Next, arm your Sparrows and steer directly toward the blinking MiG so that it's centered in the range indicator. By now you should have climbed to around 5000 feet and your speed should be Mach 1.

Enemy Sighted

Before long, a blip representing the target plane will appear on the top edge of your radar screen. This means that the MiG is 30 miles away. Continue to make small adjustments with the joystick to keep the enemy centered in your range indicator. Because there is a slight delay between your movement of the joystick and any onscreen response, you should wait a second or two after each movement to see its real effect.

As you fly toward the enemy, he'll also be tracking you and will fire a missile at around 20 miles that will show up as a small white blip on your radar screen. Don't let this distract you. When you close to around 15 miles of the MiG, the range indicator will suddenly turn black, and you should give the firebutton a quick tap to fire one of your six Sparrows. A longer press could result in the unnecessary launching of two or more missiles.

Immediately after firing, bank hard to the right. This swings both the MiG and its missile to the left on radar. When the enemy missile is directly on your left, level off. Then, as the missile begins to close in, turn hard to the left. By this time, your missile should have found its way to the enemy MiG and soon both the MiG and its missile will be gone from the screen. If, for any reason, your Sparrow misses the target, immediately arm your AIM-9 Sidewinders and try to maneuver around for another shot while continuing to avoid the enemy's missile. Remember, there's no such thing as light damage from a missile hit. Every hit means the end of your F-18. If your aircraft is struck, eject immediately.

Once the enemy MiG has been downed, either circle around a full 360 degrees or else access your top, rear, and side views to check for additional targets. Usually, the second MiG spotted earlier in the mission will be nowhere in sight. If so, head back to your carrier but keep your eyes open because the enemy could return at any time.

Target Strike

You begin the target strike mission exactly as you do the dog-fighting mission. This time, however, your target will be enemy warships cruising several miles to the south of your carrier. As you approach the target ship, keep your range indicator above the horizon, centered directly over the ship. Climb to 10,000 feet. When the enemy ship's smoke stacks become visible, push down to center the ship inside the range indicator. When the indicator turns black, squeeze off a couple of AGM-65s and peel off to the right. If you miss the target, circle around for another attempt.

Any SAMs launched from the enemy ship should be handled in the same manner as the MiG's air-to-air missiles. That is, keep turning at right angles away from the missile until you break free of its locking mechanism. Once the missile is no longer locked in on your F-18, try to put as much distance between yourself and the missile before returning to finish off the ship.

Closing In

If you run out of Mavericks and are forced to move in close for an attack with your MK-82s, approach at the same altitude (10,000 feet), but when the stacks appear, dive straight at the ship. Keep a close watch on your altimeter. When you reach 2000 feet, drop your bombs and pull straight back on the stick. After a half loop you'll be able to see the inverted horizon and you'll be heading north toward your carrier. From here, a half roll will put you upright so you can shake off any SAMs and head home.

What Goes Up Must Come Down

Although the Japanese kamikazes tried it during World War II, no one ever won a war by crash landing for their country. When you auger into the deck of an aircraft carrier, you not only destroy a perfectly good combat jet and make a real mess of the flight deck, you also buy yourself an early end to your simulation fun.

A high-altitude approach seems to work best when you're landing on the carrier. Fly toward the deck from the southwest at an altitude of about 5000 feet. Try to position your jet so that when your heading is 80 degrees, the white stripe on the carrier's landing strip appears vertical. If it seems that you're too far to the right of the carrier, head north for a while until you can turn gradually toward the carrier at the 80-degree heading described above.

Once you've aligned yourself properly with the carrier, reduce your throttle setting to 24 percent, lower your landing gear, and begin a shallow dive. As soon as you can make out a little more detail on the carrier, activate your speed break. All this time you should be making slight adjustments to keep the landing strip lined up properly. By the time the carrier's superstructure and trip wire appear, you should have lowered your altitude to 1000 feet, and your airspeed should be under

Mach .5. If everything is going according to plan, decrease your throttle again, this time to 14 percent. Pull up slightly as you pass over the stern of the ship, and push your nose down again when all you see in front of you is deck. Shut your engine completely off, and you've made it.

Usually, you'll proceed directly to the arming menu again, to reload. If this doesn't happen, it means you've landed but failed to catch the trip wire. Quickly access the control tower view and steer your plane around to the right, if it's still rolling on the deck. If your plane has already rolled to a stop, you'll have to turn your engine on again (to only 9 percent) and release the brake. Turn your jet completely around and run over the trip wire in the opposite direction. This will bring you back to the arming menu where you can select the weapons for your next flight.

6
F-15 Strike Eagle

F-15 Strike Eagle challenges your skill as a fighter pilot in seven different missions, each increasing in difficulty. The scenarios range from Vietnam in 1972 to the Persian Gulf in 1984. Your charge is to destroy your targets and return safely to base.

The F-15 is a sophisticated combat jet fighter that can attain a maximum airspeed in excess of Mach 2.5 and climb to over 60,000 feet. It's equipped with long-range radar and both infrared and radar-warning receivers to provide you with early detection of enemy fighters and missiles. The F-15 is also equipped with an active radar jammer, chaff dispenser, and flares to throw approaching missiles off the trail.

Offensive weapons on the F-15 include an M-61A1 six-barrel 20mm rotary cannon; four short-range AIM-9L Sidewinder heatseeking missiles; four medium-range AIM-7F Sparrows; and eighteen 500-lb MK-82 low-drag, general-purpose bombs bundled into six groups of three. To fly successful combat missions in the F-15, you must master not only the aerodynamics of flight, but also the use of your various weapons systems and countermeasures.

Slick Simulation

Fortunately, two things combine to make *F-15 Strike Eagle* one of the easiest simulated combat jets to master. The first is the logical control system that MicroProse designer Sid Meier has incorporated into the simulation. Pressing the R key selects the radar; F is used to drop flares; pressing B activates your bombs, and so forth. This system is so well designed that even if, in the heat of battle, you forget which key to use for a specific function, an educated guess works most of the time.

The ability to arm specific weapons prior to combat, and then to use a single joystick button to fire your rotary cannon, two types of missiles, and drop bombs, lets you keep your eyes on the target when you pull the trigger instead of searching the keyboard. Figure 6-1 is a diagram of the keyboard and the effects of keypresses.

Figure 6-1. Keyboard Controls

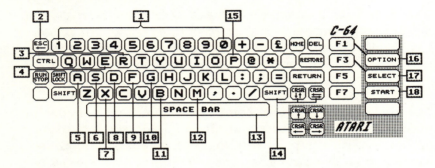

1. BACKUP THROTTLE
2. BAILOUT SWITCH
3. RADAR RANGE SELECTOR
4. ELECTRONIC COUNTER MEASURES AND CHAFF DISPENSER
5. AFTERBURNER IGNITOR SWITCH
6. SHORT RANGE MISSILE ARM SWITCH
7. SPEED BRAKE SWITCH
8. DROP TANK RELEASE
9. FLARE ACTIVATE SWITCH
10. GUN ACTIVATE SWITCH
11. BOMB ACTIVATE SWITCH
12. MEDIUM RANGE MISSILE ARM SWITCH
13. FRONT/REAR VIEW CONTROL
14. NAVIGATIONAL TARGETING CURSORS
15. PAUSE CONTROL
16. SKILL LEVEL
17. NUMBER OF PLAYERS
18. START/RESTART SWITCH

Heads Up

The second thing that helps make learning to fly combat missions in *F-15* a breeze, is the plane's superb cockpit layout. Virtually all the information you need to reach your primary targets, destroy them, and return to your home base—all without getting downed by enemy MiGs and surface-to-air missiles—is on the screen at all times. Among other things, a quick glance at the instrumentation can tell you whether you're on course to the target, whether there are any hostile planes or missiles within 160 miles, or the status of your remaining weapons. In addition, the message indicator on the Heads-Up-Display (HUD) lets you know how many gun rounds you have left, whether your bombs and missiles have destroyed their targets, and whether your plane has been damaged by enemy fire.

Although you should thoroughly familiarize yourself with the entire cockpit layout, some displays are much more useful or important than others. Obviously, the early detection of enemy planes, missiles, and ground sites, using the radar display, will give you time to take the appropriate action. Set the radar to long range at the start of a mission and leave it. Try not to let the enemy get close enough to make punching up the short-range radar necessary.

Also important are the four warning indicators above the radar display. Since these aren't labeled onscreen, study your *Flight Operations Manual* until you know precisely what each one means.

Orientation

The Horizontal Situation Display (HSD) shows the locations of your home base, the primary target(s), all SAM installations, the enemy's military airports, and the position and heading of your F-15. Learn to use the HSD's navigation cursor to set your flight paths to specific targets. The cursor's response to keyboard input can be sluggish at times, so give it a second or two to respond to each keystroke. Once it's on target, find the steering cue on the HUD and fly into it to reach your target. Don't forget that this system can also be used to guide you home.

Don't be like Clint Eastwood and forget whether you've fired three Sidewinders or four. Learn to read your Weapons Status Display (WSD), and you'll always know exactly how many AIM-9L and AIM-7F missiles are still strapped beneath your wings. This display will also keep you informed of the number of MK-82s and flares you have left, and whether or not you've dropped the external fuel tanks.

Finally, keep an eye on the altimeter. While pursuing or

trying to lose enemy MiGs, it's easy to lose track of your altitude. Bombing ground targets or even returning to base is impossible when you're up in the stratosphere, so don't climb when you should be in level flight. At the other extreme, low-altitude flight can cause your F-15 to become unstable, so be sure to maintain an altitude of at least 2000 feet when you're not in the process of dive bombing or evading enemy radar and missile installations.

Other instruments, such as the HUD heading, mach indicator, and engine power indicator aren't as important as long as you know you're on course and are maintaining sufficient airspeed. Get in the habit of giving the entire cockpit a quick scan once in a while to make sure everything is under control.

More Gas

One instrument that isn't half as important as most people think is the Fuel Status Display. While most pilots cruise at around 90-percent throttle, and reserve their powerful afterburner for emergencies, to save fuel, a little-known glitch in the program actually allows you to use the afterburner as much as you want while expending fuel only as fast as you would at the lowest throttle setting.

Although your *Flight Operations Manual* states that the F-15's afterburner increases fuel consumption by 60 percent over the rate at 100-percent throttle, in practice, the afterburner actually eats up your jet fuel no faster than the throttle setting in effect, right before you turned it on. By setting your throttle at 55 percent immediately before you ignite the afterburner, you can cruise to your target and pursue enemy MiGs at speeds in excess of Mach 1.5, while expending fuel only one quarter as fast as you would at 100 percent throttle. If you remember to conserve fuel with this technique, you'll probably never have to worry about the low fuel indicator lighting, and you'll rarely find it necessary to drop empty external fuel tanks.

What happens if your fuel tanks do run dry miles from base and your air speed begins to plummet—followed closely by your F-15? Do you panic and hit the bail-out switch? No way. Just set the navigation cursor on your base and give the afterburner switch a tap. Nothing happens you say? Hit it again. In fact, keep tapping it and watch your airspeed start to climb to as much as 1680 knots. This will let you make it safely back to base or, if you're real adventurous, simply continue the mission. Be warned, however, that any joystick movement while you're tapping a throttle key can be misinterpreted by the computer and cause unpredictable results. Since several keystrokes can be stored in the keyboard buffer after you've stopped tapping the key, make sure the last keystroke has registered before you move the stick.

★★ Level: Pilot ★★
Mission 4: Syria, March 12, 1984

To fulfill this mission, you must make repeated raids against Syrian SAM installations and military airfields as you work your way northeast to the primary ground target, the air command center in Damascus. If, at any time in the course of the mission, your F-15 is damaged by enemy fire or your arms supply runs dangerously low, return immediately to the home base in Haifa, Israel. Figure 6-2 is a map of the area.

You can expect heavy resistance from Syrian fighters equipped with air-to-air heatseeking missiles. Through a series of quick strikes, you'll be able to wear down Syria's defenses gradually to the point where one final bombing raid will eliminate the primary target.

MiGs

As the mission begins, you find yourself airborne at around 10,000 feet and in a perfect position to hammer an enemy MiG. Before you do anything else, fire a burst of 25 shells (one squeeze of the trigger) from your 20mm rotary cannon to insure a first hit. You'll need two more hits to down the MiG, so stay right on his tail. (He usually tries to break off the engagement by pulling up and to the right, so be prepared to react accordingly.) Immediately after the third hit, activate your long-range radar, place your navigation cursor on the SAM site that's directly east of your home base, and align your air-to-air reticle with the flashing N-A-V steering cue.

Figure 6-2. Map of Syria (Mission 4)

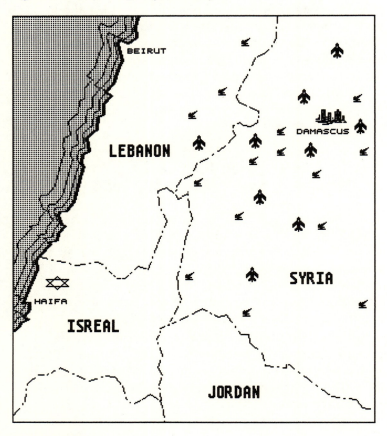

Once you're on course and cruising toward the ground target, push down into a shallow dive to lose altitude slowly as you approach the SAM site. Ideally, you'll want to be flying at an altitude of 3500–5000 feet when the ground target first appears on long-range radar. Arm a medium-range missile and be prepared to fire as soon as the air target designator box appears on the HUD. This signifies that one or more enemy MiGs have been sent up to welcome you. Don't even wait to pick up the MiGs on radar before you fire. If two MiGs attack simultaneously, arm a short-range missile while the first missile finds its way to the target. By the time the first MiG has been hit, the second will be close enough to destroy with the short-range missile. If the second MiG manages to avoid the missile, be prepared to do a little dogfighting with your rotary cannons. Just don't waste so much time playing cat and mouse with the MiGs that you forget about your ground target.

Missiles

When the HSD shows that you're about to fly over the SAM site, extend your speed brake and activate your air-to-ground reticle to arm your bombs. If the radar or infrared warning indicators light at any time, use the appropriate countermeasures—either ECM jamming or flares—to reduce the risk of an enemy missile finding you. Remember, the first indicator light on the left warns of radar tracking; when it lights, you should respond by jamming and releasing chaff. The indicator beside it signifies infrared tracking—a heatseeking missile on the way—and you should drop a flare or two.

As soon as the SAM site appears on radar, try to spot it through the cockpit window. When you see it, maintain visual contact as you maneuver your F-15 to position the bombing reticle in the center of the target. This usually means pushing into an even steeper dive. Release your bombs and pull up out of the dive. Then reignite your afterburner, remembering first to cut the throttle to 55 percent to save fuel. You'll want to climb to at least 2500 feet to avoid low-altitude turbulence and restore more stable control of your aircraft.

If a "Bombs Miss" message appears, you can often get a

second chance at the ground target by pulling up into a half-loop so that you're flying inverted. Arm your bombs, align the air-to-ground reticle as you normally would, and let them drop. Not only is this a lot faster than a second approach after a wide-banking turn, but this maneuver will put you in a much better position to shoot down any MiGs that were on your tail during the first pass.

If both you and your F-15 are still in one piece when the red flash from below signifies that the bomb was on target, and if your WSD still shows one or two AIM-7s on board, move your navigation cursor onto the airport that's to the north of the SAM site you just obliterated, and eliminate it in the same manner.

Since the F-15 carries only four medium and four short-range missiles, it's easy to get caught deep behind enemy lines without any missiles. Once you've fired your last AIM-7F Sparrow, begin the return flight to your home base. Sidewinders can be effective even against MiGs that are on your tail, so be sure to save at least one for the trip back.

In this, and in other *F-15* missions where primary targets are far from your base and heavily defended, don't try to be a hero and complete the mission in a single flight. A more effective strategy is to divide the mission into several flights, eliminating as many SAM installations and military airports as is safely possible in each flight. This way, you can gradually clear a path directly to your primary targets. Not only does this make your final strike against the primary target go much smoother, but once you shake that last troublesome missile or MiG that decides to follow you home, it's usually clear flying for the rest of the return trip.

7
Gunship

Considered the West's finest attack helicopter, the AH-64A Apache is more like a flying tank than a flying machine. In your Gunship, fly missions under battlefire from Vietnam to Central America.

The AH-64A Apache was designed to provide support for friendly ground forces against armored vehicles and antiaircraft artillery. One of the Apache's great strengths is its ability, by hovering close to the ground, to approach enemy positions, remaining undetected. It can then pop up—from behind a hill, a building, or trees—just long enough to launch a Hellfire missile or two. If necessary, the Apache can fly at close to 200 mph and climb to over 20,000 feet.

Equipment
The Apache comes with a 30mm *chain gun* as standard equipment. This automatic cannon has a maximum capacity of 1200 High-Explosive Dual Purpose (HEDP) rounds that it fires at a rate of 625 per minute. The real Apache uses a sophisticated Target Acquisition and Designation System (TADS), which lets the pilot and gunner aim the chain gun simply by looking at the target. This system requires that both men wear special IHADSS helmets, which are tracked in three dimensions by infrared sensors built into the cockpit. While *Gunship* doesn't come with an IHADSS helmet that you can strap on when you play the simulation, it does use a sophisticated aiming system that can automatically lock onto targets within your line of sight.

In addition to the standard chain gun, some of the other

weapons with which you can equip your simulated Apache include AGM-114A Hellfire missiles, 2.75-inch FFAR rockets, and AIM-9L Sidewinders missiles. Since each of these is most effective against a specific type of target, your weapons mix—the type and number of each—will depend on the kinds of targets you'll be required to destroy and the types of enemy forces you expect to encounter in a mission. Weight limitations imposed by weather conditions may also affect the total number of weapons your helicopter can carry. You can also select other requirements—like fuel, chaff, flares, and HEDP rounds—at the start of a mission, or by landing at friendly bases while the mission is in progress.

Instrumentation

Once airborne, you can monitor your supply of rockets, rounds, missiles, chaff, and flares by keeping an eye on the Stores Selection display. This not only shows the number of each type of offensive and defensive stores remaining, but also tells you the one that's currently armed and ready. When a flare or chaff decoy is used, its Stores Selection indicator remains lit as long as the defense is functioning.

Much of the rest of the Apache's cockpit display consists of the usual assortment of gauges and indicators that you'd find in any aircraft. These include a compass (both rotary and digital), airspeed indicator, altimeter, vertical speed indicator, artificial horizon, and fuel gauge (see Figure 7-1). Of these, only the artificial horizon can be safely ignored. Everything else must be monitored with varying frequency during flight. For example, since much of your flying will be done relatively close to the ground, you should keep an eye on the altimeter at all times. On the other hand, something like the vertical speed indicator only has to be watched closely while landing.

The cockpit is also home to a number of high-tech extras like radar, infrared warning lights, and jammers to help you avoid radar-guided and heatseeking missiles, an INS destination indicator that guides you to the target chosen on the computerized sector map, an automatic dual-range threat display, and a small video screen in the center of the panel.

Figure 7-1. AH-64A Apache Instrument Panel

You can use this screen in three ways, depending on the situation. When the TADS locks onto a target, the screen provides you with a close-up of the target along with a digital readout of its range in kilometers. When a radio message is broadcast, it can be read using the display. And at all other times, the video screen displays a small portion of the large sector map, centered on your helicopter.

Along the top of the cockpit are 14 system damage lights corresponding to the Apache's major systems—nose optics, avionics bays, engines, weapons wings, and so on. When a system is damaged, its system damage light turns from green to yellow; it changes to red if the system is destroyed. Figure 7-2 lists the damage warning lights (which run across the very top of the instrument screen).

Weaponry

Your AH-64A Apache helicopter can carry a variety of offensive weapons into battle. Not only is each weapon most effective against a specific kind of target, but each has its own range and method of aiming. To be a successful *Gunship* pilot,

Figure 7-2. Damage Warning Lights

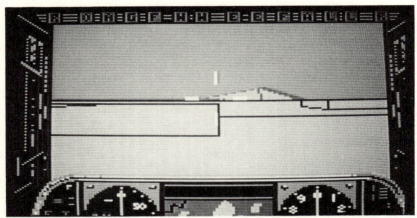

At top, left to right:

R   Main rotor

O   Nose optics (controls TADS)

A   Forward avionics bay

G   Chain gun (30mm cannon)

F   Forward fuel tank

W   Port weapons wing

W   Starboard weapons wing

E   Port engine

E   Starboard engine

F   Aft fuel tank

A   Aft avionics bay

L   Chaff decoy launcher

L   Flare decoy launcher

R   Tail rotor (controls rotation)

you must learn the strengths and limitations of each weapon. There's nothing worse than mistakenly firing your last Sidewinder heatseeking missile at an enemy bunker, only to spot a Russian-built Hind helicopter on the threat display, closing in for the kill.

Here's a rundown of the Apache's weapons systems, along with suitable targets, special notes on aiming, and effective range.

30mm Chain Gun

Targets. While the rapid-firing chain gun doesn't have the range of your missiles and rockets, it's useful against most types of air and ground targets including helicopters, infantry, self-propelled surface-to-air missile launchers, antiaircraft guns, armored personnel carriers, tanks, depots, helibases, headquarters, and missile launchers. Bunkers will take several hits from the chain gun before being destroyed, but if you're out of Hellfire missiles and have several HEDP rounds to spare, go ahead and give the bunker a spray—especially if it's your primary or secondary target.

Aiming. Another advantage of the chain gun is that it doesn't have to be aimed manually. As long as a target is within your line of sight, the TADS can lock onto it and aim the gun for you. When you're under attack, you can continue to pound a target even while you're flying evasively.

Range. 0.7–1.5 km.

AGM-114A Hellfires

Targets. The Hellfire's armor-penetrating capability makes it very effective against bunkers and all types of armored vehicles. The Hellfire's punch is very concentrated, however. Consequently, it's less effective against infantry, antiaircraft guns, helibases, depots, and other structures.

Aiming. Since you can continue to steer Hellfires toward the target once they've been launched, you don't have to wait until you have the target perfectly lined up before you fire. As soon as the TADS gunsight is anywhere close to the fixed crosshairs of your cockpit window, let the Hellfire fly. Then carefully guide it to the target. If it's off course, say to the left, don't try to correct the missile's flight path by simply aiming at the target. You should overcompensate by aiming to the right of the target. This will make the Hellfire slide across and into the target.

Range. 3–6km.

2.75-inch FFAR Rockets

Targets. Although Folding-Fin Aerial Rockets (thus, the FFAR) don't have as much power and, therefore, can't punch through heavily armored targets like Hellfires, they fragment upon impact. That makes them effective against infantry, anti-aircraft guns, helibases, depots, and other installations.

Aiming. These rockets are unguided. Once you've re-leased the FFAR, then, don't waste time watching it to the tar-get—it doesn't do any good. Instead, select another target immediately, or take another shot at the same target.

Range. 1.8km.

AIM-9L Sidewinders

Targets. These heatseeking missiles have only one use—to destroy enemy Hind helicopters. This, they do effectively as long as they're not jammed or decoyed.

Aiming. Always try to spot Hinds as soon as they enter the threat display. (They appear as red and white flashing dots.) If you see one, turn to face it, lock in with the TADS system, and fire. Sidewinders have a long range, so don't wait until the enemy's on top of you before firing.

Range. 18km.

Mission Strategy

After completing your *Gunship* training in the United States, you'll have a choice of mission location—Southeast Asia, Central America, the Middle East, or Western Europe. Although your *Operations Manual* suggests starting in Southeast Asia or Central America—because these areas lack the sophisticated equipment found in the Middle East and western Europe—the program's style and reality options let you customize the struggle in any area to suit your level of experience. For example, while the Warsaw Pact forces in western Europe have the most sophisticated weapons, including ZSU-30-2 antiair-craft guns and SA-13 self-propelled SAM (Surface-to-Air Missile) launchers, these weapons are only available to their first-line troops. By selecting third-line troops and flying the regular rather than the volunteer mission, you should be able to take on enemy forces in any part of the world.

No Two Alike

One of the things that makes *Gunship* so exciting, but also so difficult to master, is that no two missions are exactly alike. That's true even if the duty, style, and reality settings are identical. One time you might be called upon to support a friendly base or troops, and the next time up you'll be given the location of depot or helibase to eliminate. Other times, your instructions will simply be to search and destroy all enemy targets in a specific area. No matter what your instructions are, there are several things to keep in mind that will help make your mission a success.

Climb Up

First of all, the map you see before starting the mission shows only the locations of your primary and secondary targets. Other enemy forces won't appear on the map until they've been spotted with TADS. When you start a mission, it's usually a good idea to climb a couple hundred feet straight above your helibase and rotate left or right a full 360 degrees, to identify any enemy forces that may be in the area. The higher you climb, the more you'll be able to see. Unfortunately, the higher your altitude, the more visible you'll be to enemy radar, so you may want to only climb high enough to check the immediate area. Return to the map and move the navigation cursor onto the first major threat that stands between you and one of your assigned targets.

Keep Low

As you head toward the enemy, stay low and keep your eyes open for TARGET warnings on the CRT message display. Near your own base, most of these will be friendly tanks and troops. Nevertheless, identify each potential threat immediately by pressing the joystick button once. Then, if it's a friendly target, press the Shift key to check for enemy forces in the same line of vision. Similarly, if you spot an enemy target, but one which poses little real threat (such as a bunker or depot), check for more dangerous targets like antiaircraft guns or self-propelled SAM launchers. Remember, most enemy installations are heavily defended. In particular, keep in mind that in places like Southeast Asia, the artillery is optically guided and won't trigger your radar or infrared warning systems.

Keep Calm

If you spot a number of approaching missiles on the threat display, don't panic. Steer your way clear until the display changes to the short-range mode. This happens automatically when the approaching missiles are close enough. The view in the long-range mode is too cluttered and is the wrong place for you to try to outmaneuver missiles. Fortunately, your gunship is heavily armored and can often take several hits before you're in real danger.

Sooner or later, however, your Apache is bound to take a devastating hit that knocks out your engines. When this happens, you can't just bail out of the machine (helicopter pilots don't wear parachutes anyway). Instead, perform an *autorotation*, a maneuver that lets you land hard, but at least in one piece.

If you've never tried an autorotation before (perhaps because the description in your *Operation Manual* sounded complicated), don't worry. All you need to remember are two things. First, as soon as enemy fire kills your engines, disengage your rotor. The sooner you do this, the greater the likelihood you'll survive. Second, after gaining control of your craft so that it's dropping rapidly but level, wait until the helicopter is down to around 100 feet, then pull back on the stick as you tap the *up fast* collective key for all you're worth. Unless you're very close to the ground when hit, this autorotation should let you walk away from the crash landing nine times out of ten.

Fight Another Day

Gunship missions don't have to be completed in just one flight. If your Apache suffers damage that directly affects its performance or your ability to carry out the mission, return to the nearest friendly base for repairs. If you've already taken out one of the assigned targets, however, be ready to respond with the appropriate countersign when the U.S. base broadcasts the password. Be sure either to check your *Gunship Operations Manual* and write down the appropriate countersign at the start of each mission, or refer to the list of passwords and countersigns in Table 7-1.

Table 7-1. *Gunship* Passwords and Countersigns

Accent/Trampoline	Billboard/Kickback
Cromagnon/Melodrama	Dakota/Onstage
Electra/Vertical	Foothold/Insolent
Grenadier/Nocturne	Hedgehog/Locksmith
Ivory/Willow	Knockout/Purebred
Lozenge/Romantic	Mazurka/Yellow
Nebula/Quaker	Ovation/Upstage
Penthouse/Symphony	Quartz/Zebra

★ PART 2 ★

IN THE WAR ROOM
(Strategic and Tactical Simulations)

★ SECTION 1 ★
NAVAL BATTLES

8
Broadsides

Take the helm of a Napoleonic sailing ship and get an authentic look at the way sea battles were waged in the days before radar, sonar, and harpoon-guided missiles.

★★ Option D ★★
USS *Constitution* vs. HMS *Guerriere*

Although *Broadsides* offers both an arcade and tactical level of play, the only real difference between the games is the number of variables you're allowed to control during battle. The arcade game, for example, lets you use only solid shot for ammunition, while the tactical game gives you a choice of solid shot, grape shot, or chain shot. What's more, although you can steer the ship, accelerate, decelerate, or maintain a constant speed during the arcade game, only the tactical version allows you actually to adjust the rigging of your ship's sails.

With both games, your options are presented on a command display at the top of the screen, and either the keyboard or a joystick can be used to cycle through the available commands. The problem with this interface is that, often, you'll waste a lot of valuable time trying to locate the option you wish to select. A better system would have used separate indicators to represent the status of the ship's systems (sails, ammunition, and so forth) and a different key to control each. This would have made the game slightly more difficult to learn, but in the long run, it would have been easier to play. Despite this sometimes awkward control scheme, five years after its initial release, *Broadsides* remains an enjoyable simulation.

Getting Your Sea Legs

Commanding a sail-powered wooden battleship during the Napoleonic era was quite different from being at the helm of one of today's modern warships, or even commanding a Fletcher-class destroyer during the Second World War. Instead of simply ordering flank speed ahead and feeling the immediate surge of response from the ship's engines, captains of ships like the *Victory*, the *Constellation*, and the *Bonhomme Richard* depended on the concerted effort of a skilled crew and the kindness of ocean winds to carry them into battle. Likewise, to be a successful *Broadsides* skipper, you have to learn to use your sails and the wind to outmaneuver your enemy during battle.

Turning the ship to either port (left) or starboard (right) is accomplished in 30-degree intervals by moving your joystick in the desired direction and pressing the firebutton, or by using the appropriate computer keys. Depending on the turning speed of the particular ship you command, each 30-degree turn will take from 1½ to almost 4 game minutes. Similarly, changes in rigging should be planned well in advance since each change can take from 30 seconds to almost 3 minutes from the moment the order is issued to be completed.

You start each game with your rigging set at Battle Sail, but you can cut your ship's speed in half by ordering Back Sail or double your ship's maximum speed by ordering Full Sail. You should be aware, however, that sails at full sail can suffer twice as much damage when hit by enemy fire as sails at battle sail. For this reason, new players may want to leave their rigging set at Battle Sail and simply use the Faster Speed, Slower Speed, and Steady Speed commands to control the speed of the ship. Then, once you have learned to maneuver your wooden battleship like a sleek racing yacht, you'll be able to hoist up the full sails and cruise into battle at double the normal speed.

Shootout on the High Seas

Broadside's tactical game lets you use three types of ammunition—solid shot, grape shot, and chain shot. Besides selecting your ammunition, you also get to aim your cannons at either the enemy's hull or his sails. You are awarded points for damaging either of these areas, as well as for destroying the enemy's cannons and killing opposing crew members. Unless you specifically need to slow your opponent's ship, however, you should aim at his hull throughout most of the battle, since this will allow you to hit all targets except sails.

Keep in mind that at the start of a game, your cannons are aimed at your opponent's sails and are loaded with solid shot. Think of solid shot as your basic cannonballs. Although they will cause some damage to sails, they are used primarily to blast holes in the enemy's hull. The ammo of choice for shredding your opponent's sails is *chain shot.* When firing chain shot, be sure you're within 700 yards of the enemy's ship—that's this ammo's maximum range. Also, bear in mind that when you're less than 125 yards from the enemy's ship, you'll be able to hit only his hull, and chain shot can do nothing to damage the enemy's hull.

Finally, grape shot is the most effective type of ammunition for killing crew members aboard the enemy's ship. Therefore, before attempting to board the opponent's ship, you should load up with grape shot to thin out his crew. Just remember first to close to within 400 yards of the enemy; then aim your cannons at his hull and fire away.

Ammo Restrictions

Now, besides knowing which type of shot to use in each situation, you should also be aware of the loading and aiming restrictions associated with each of these three types of ammunition. First, no matter what loading or aiming command you issue, your command will affect only the guns on the side of the ship that is closest to the enemy. Thus, your starboard cannons may be loaded with solid shot and aimed at the enemy's hull at the same time your port cannons are blasting away at the enemy's sails with chain shot. However, only those cannons on the side closest to the enemy ship are used when you give the order to fire.

69

Second, you should always load your ammunition before changing your aim, or your command may be ignored. For example, if you are currently firing chain shot at your enemy's sails and would like to begin attacking his hull with solid shot, you must load the solid shot before trying to take aim at the enemy's hull. Otherwise, the order to change your aim will have no effect. Likewise, since grape shot can be fired only at the opponent's hull, any order to aim at the enemy's sails while your cannons are packed with grape shot will be ignored until either solid shot or chain shot has been loaded.

All Aboard

One of the most exciting elements of *Broadsides* is the possibility of boarding the enemy's ship to settle your differences at close range. This is often your best option when you find yourself outgunned or simply outmaneuvered by a faster ship (particularly if you have a much larger crew than your opponent). Once the two ships have been secured together with grappling lines, it's up to your swordfighting ability and the accuracy of your snipers to win the battle.

Figure 8-1. Boarding Screen

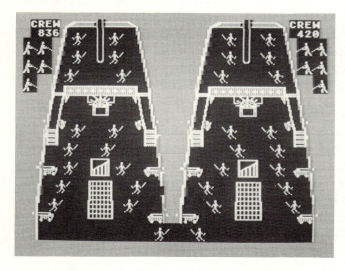

During a boarding, enter all commands through the keyboard. Your onscreen swordfighter is controlled by using only five basic moves. These are a move to the left, a move to the right, a thrust, a counterthrust, and a hack. While swordfighting, your crew suffers casualties in proportion to the effectiveness with which you wield your sword. Figure 8-1 shows the boarding screen.

Hand to Hand

When you're trying to develop an effective swordfighting strategy, two things should be kept in mind—the relative strength of each of the three moves, and the number of enemy crew members killed when each move "hits." First, as the player manual explains, the counterthrust beats the thrust, the thrust beats the hack, and the hack beats the counterthrust. Second, beating your opponent with a hack kills six men compared with four men for the thrust and just two for the counterthrust. Considering the relative strengths of each sword movement and the casualty rates that result from beating your opponent with each move, it's easy to conclude that you should rely almost exclusively on the thrust and the hack, while only rarely using the counterthrust. Here's why.

Assuming that the chances of your opponent picking any one of the three moves are even, as long as you stick to the thrust or the hack, your opponent will lose an average of two more men than you for every three sword movements the two of you make. The reason is that if he counterthrusts while you thrust, you lose two men; if he thrusts while you thrust, you both lose four men; and if he hacks while you thrust, he loses four men. Consequently, this series of three exchanges results in your opponent's losing eight men while you lose only six. Thus, if your opponent uses the three attacking moves with roughly the same frequency, you'll come out on top. Although the math is slightly different, the results of your continued use of the hack would be the same. However, in these same conditions, your exclusive use of the counterthrust would result in your losing an average of four more men than your opponent for every three exchanges.

The number of kills resulting from a clash of swords is

also affected by the foot movement of the two swordsmen. When you're moving toward the enemy, your casualties will be doubled if you find yourself on the losing end of an exchange. If you retreat, however, both your casualty rates and the number of enemy crew members you kill with a successful hack, thrust, or counterthrust will be halved. Therefore, assuming you'll win a majority of the exchanges, it's usually best to let the enemy come to you.

Between swordfighting rounds, snipers perched in the rigging of your ship use their pistols to shoot at the enemy. Your five snipers, each representing 10 men, may be ordered to fire at snipers on the enemy ship, enemies on the deck of the opponent's ship, or enemies that have boarded your own ship. In most circumstances, it's best to order all of your snipers to fire at enemies on the opponent's deck since the chances of hitting enemy snipers is slim, and firing down at your own deck can result in some of your own men getting caught in the crossfire.

Strategy and Tactics

Having lived just a few blocks from the permanent home of the USS *Constitution* for over 20 years, and having boarded the wooden battle ship on occasion to view its silent cannons and carronades, I naturally chose Option D as the scenario for discussion in this chapter. Option D pits "Old Ironsides" against the British *Guerriere*, and although the ships are fairly evenly matched, the *Constitution* does have a few distinct advantages.

Pluses and Minuses

First, the *Constitution* is a slightly faster ship with a starting speed of 3.4 knots compared with 3.1 knots for the *Guerriere*. Its loading time is 10 game seconds quicker than that of the *Guerriere*, and, perhaps most important, the time it takes the *Constitution* to make a 30-degree turn is a full 20 seconds less than the turning time of the *Guerriere*. This is important since it allows the player commanding the *Constitution* to outmaneuver the opponent through a series of quick turns.

Also notable is the difference in crew sizes between the

two ships—420 men aboard the *Constitution* compared with only 270 for the *Guerriere*. Because one of the ways a player can lose is by having his or her crew reduced to one-fourth its original size, the player commanding the *Constitution* must kill only slightly over 200 of the *Guerriere*'s men to win, while the captain of the *Guerriere* must kill 315 of the *Constitution*'s crew.

Another advantage that the player commanding the *Constitution* has over the opponent, is the *Constitution*'s sturdier hull, which will keep the ship afloat through 70 hits (the *Guerriere* sinks after only 50 hits). This advantage in hull strength is offset, however, by the *Guerriere*'s superior shot damage rating. When on target, the British ship will inflict 10 percent more hits than the standard number, and the *Constitution* inflicts 10 percent fewer.

Finally, the *Constitution*'s snipers are nearly twice as accurate as those aboard the *Guerriere*. This greater accuracy, when taken into consideration with the *Constitution*'s larger crew size, makes the overall strategy for winning the scenario obvious: Use your greater speed to chase down and catch the *Guerriere* as quickly as possible, board the enemy ship, and aggressively battle your opponent with your sword and your snipers.

Therefore, as soon as the battle begins, pack your cannons with grape shot and aim at the *Guerriere*'s hull. Then set your sails to full, and turn your ship 30 degrees toward the enemy. Continue to blast away with grape shot until you are close enough to board the enemy ship.

Once aboard, use the swordfighting and sniping tactics previously described to chip away at the enemy crew. Since the opposing captain usually retreats back onto his own deck during the swordfights, you'll always have to be on the offensive. Once the enemy reaches his own grating, however, stop advancing and let him come to you. That way, when you hit, you'll kill twice as many men. When the number of enemy crew members drops to below 67, the *Guerriere* will surrender, and victory will be yours.

9
Carriers at War

In World War II, the Battle of Midway was an important point in changing Allied fortunes in the Pacific sea war. Carriers at War is notable for its depth of historical detail and for its unique menu-driven orders phase. In the scenario described here, you take on the role of Admiral Ray Spruance, commanding task force 16. Your job is to prevent the invasion of Midway.

★★ Scenario ★★
Midway, June 3–6, 1942 (Spruance Command)

On the night of June 3, 1942, the Japanese were preparing to attack the U.S. base on the small Pacific island of Midway. By invading Midway, the Japanese hoped to lure the U.S. fleet to within striking distance of their carrier-based fighter squadrons. It was a desperate move, and one that ultimately backfired. The first strike began with 108 aircraft from the Japanese carrier force attacking the island. These forces were met by U.S. fighters, which were promptly massacred in the ensuing air battles. Nevertheless, the U.S. defenders were successful in keeping damage on the island to a minimum.

Immediately, the Japanese began preparing for a second strike against Midway. By this time, however, the U.S. carrier force had located the Japanese carriers and, before a second Japanese strike could be launched, American carrier planes began heading for the IJN carrier force.

The first U.S. planes to arrive, a group of 41 torpedo bombers, were almost all destroyed and did virtually no damage to the Japanese carriers. However, the arrival of the U.S.

dive bombers turned the tide of battle, and in a matter of minutes, three Japanese carriers—the *Akagi*, *Kaga*, and *Soryu*—were hit and sinking. With them went scores of zeros and the skilled pilots who would have flown them in the second Midway attack.

A fourth Japanese carrier, the *Hiryu*, was also sunk by American carrier planes, but not before it had launched a successful strike against the damaged U.S. carrier *Yorktown*. Three days later, the *Yorktown* was finished off by a Japanese submarine.

Despite the loss of the *Yorktown* and several American pilots and planes, the Battle of Midway is considered one of the most decisive victories by the U.S. Navy during World War II. When it was over, the Japanese were left with only two large carriers, and America's strategic position in the Pacific had greatly improved.

Carriers at War was the first war game released by the Australia-based Strategic Studies Group (SSG).

Since the *Carriers at War* manual recommends the Spruance command for the Allied player, this is the one I've chosen for discussion here. Before setting your task force in motion, however, you should become familiar with some of the more important reports and tactical options available through the *Carriers at War* system of menus.

War Gaming à la Carte

By selecting Orders from the Game menu, you can check reports on both Axis and Allied damage and losses, locate the task groups under your command and issue general orders, or locate individual carriers and order their squadrons into action. If you elect to read your battle reports, you'll notice that information on the enemy's losses is limited, while data concerning your own forces is detailed and extensive.

Both reports begin with a victory screen that summarizes the number and types of ships and aircraft that have been lost or damaged, those remaining active, and the victory points awarded for losses so far. However, the report on your own forces goes on for several screen pages to detail the specific damage and losses to your land bases, carriers, and their planes. The final section of your battle report lists the damage level of every ship in your entire task force including all carriers, capital warships, subs, minor warships, and auxiliary vessels. Although, admittedly, once heavy losses begin showing up here, there's little that can be done except to pull back the affected forces and try to regroup before sailing back into battle.

Besides records of Allied and Axis damage and losses, you can also call up reports on sightings of enemy aircraft squadrons, task groups, and land bases, as well as reports on the status of any friendly air strikes in progress. Both the Sighted and Strike reports use icons to identify the locations of air squadrons, task groups, and land bases on the battle map. By cycling through the icons with cursor keys, you can access additional information on each one.

Giving Orders

Once you've read all the reports and are ready to issue some orders, there are two action menus you must use to issue general movement orders to your task groups and order specific air strikes to be launched from your carriers. By selecting Group from the Naval Commander menu, you can cycle through the task groups under your command according to the way they are identified on the battle map and choose the one you wish to examine.

Task groups that haven't been designated for involuntary missions, such as transport, bombard, or refuel may be assigned to a strike, escort, support, or cover mission. In most cases, however, a group's mission should remain the one assigned to it during scenario creation. Task groups without a specific object can be given a heading and a speed at which to travel. When an enemy task group is spotted, you may engage it in surface-to-surface combat by designating it as the objective of the task group that located it. Once such an objective has been assigned, there's no need to set a new heading for your task group, manually, as it will automatically cruise toward the enemy task group.

You may also order your carrier-based squadrons to attack any enemy task groups that have been spotted and that are within range. The first step toward launching a strike is locating the friendly carrier that will serve as the base of operations. Strikes may then be ordered directly from the Set Strike Routine menu by assigning available bomber squadrons to strike, and by assigning available fighters to escort them to the target. Strikes may further be designated as either cohesive or individual. Although cohesive strikes take longer to form and reach the target, they provide better protection for your bombers by insuring that all squadrons in the strike force remain together as they approach the target, and then return.

One way to speed up the process of preparing and launching a strike is by readying your squadrons in advance via the Set Order Routine menu. Just be sure to launch a strike quickly, once your squadrons have been readied, or fatigue could set in before they even get off the ground.

Strategy and Tactics

As Admiral Ray Spruance, you have been given command of Task Force 16. Your job is to prevent the invasion of Midway by the IJN through bomber attacks on the Japanese fleet. In the actual battle, Spruance's task force disabled ten Japanese ships, including the four carriers mentioned earlier. As a result of his leadership at Midway, Spruance was appointed chief of staff to Admiral Nimitz. While there's no promotion in it for you, foiling the Japanese invasion plans while keeping your own fleet intact will prove you've got what it takes to lead a carrier force into battle.

The task force you command is made up of four smaller task groups with flagships, *Enterprise*, *Yorktown*, CA32, and DD390. Both the *Enterprise* and *Yorktown* groups have been assigned Strike missions and will be escorted into battle by the CA32 group. The task group headed by DD390 is included for historical accuracy, but has little real use in the scenario because it was assigned to a refueling mission during the creation of the scenario, and these orders can't be changed.

When the scenario opens, it is 2100 hours on the night of June 3, 1942. The three main task groups under your command are positioned about 240 nautical miles to the northeast of Midway Island and are heading southwest at a speed of 15 knots. A quick check of the weather report reveals that, although clouds and squalls cover much of the eastern part of the map, the area around Midway is mostly clear.

While none of the IJN task groups have yet been located by your carriers, air reconnaissance out of Midway has pinpointed Vice Admiral Nagumo's task force about 540 nautical miles west of the *Yorktown* task group. However, no strikes can be launched until your task groups' search planes have sighted the enemy carriers and your squadrons have been readied for the strike. Therefore, you should set the speed of your three main task groups to 30 knots and change the headings of the *Yorktown* and *Enterprise* task groups to west. Because the CA32 group has been assigned to escort the *Enterprise* group, it will automatically try to remain within the same hex.

Then, select one of your three carriers and call up the Plane Status Display. As you'll see, all of your planes are dispersed and must be armed before any strikes can be launched. This is done by choosing the Select Order Routine and cycling through and readying each of your squads in turn. Once you've readied every squad on the first carrier, be sure to do the same for the squads on both of the other carriers. This will start all of your planes moving from the hangar to the arming area and, eventually, to the flight deck for takeoff. Finally, return to the Game menu and set your task force into action by selecting Run.

First Attack

The clock will begin running and for the next several game hours your task groups will sail to the west. The first waves of enemy planes will begin attacking Midway at about 4:00 a.m., but the island's computer-controlled defenses will help to keep damage on the island to a minimum. Once your ships have located the first Japanese task group, the clock will stop (usually around 8:00 a.m. on June 4). This may be the time to send out the first counterstrike.

Select the carrier *Yorktown*, and before issuing any orders, stop by the Plane Status Display. Note that all of the planes that were dispersed last night have now reached the arming stage. Go to the Set Strike menu and, if you are close enough to the enemy task group, arm fighter squadrons 5 and 6 for escort and bomber squadrons 13, 14, and 20 for strike. In addition, by ordering a cohesive strike, you will insure that all of the squadron will fly at a uniform speed to the objective, and that your bombers will receive maximum protection from your fighters.

Since several more enemy task groups are in the area, don't launch any strikes from either the *Hornet* or the *Enterprise* at this point. Instead, return to the Game menu and let some more time click off the clock. Before long, you'll spot a second Japanese task group. This time, send up a cohesive strike made up of fighter squadrons 9 and 10 and bomber squads 18, 19, and 22 from the *Hornet*. Again, keep the *Enterprise* on deck—within the next hour, a third enemy task group will be spotted and, this time, it will be Nagumo's carrier group.

Time is now of the essence. Instead of a cohesive strike, arm the *Enterprise*'s two fighter squadrons for escort and the three bomber squadrons for an extended strike with armor-piercing bombs. Unlike the cohesive strikes from the *Hornet* and *Yorktown*, these strikes will get underway within minutes. By noon, the first battle reports should begin coming in.

Strike and Pause

Once your squadrons begin returning to their carriers, let them rest in the dispersed station for as long as possible to avoid unnecessary fatigue. If you attempt to keep all of your squadrons in the ready state and launch repeated strikes until the sun goes down, you'll soon find that very few squadrons will be available for strike selection.

As the day wears on, the Japanese will take a long time to continue their aggressive operations (especially if your earlier strikes were successful). Therefore, let the hours tick by, but keep a close watch on enemy task groups that are spotted, paying close attention to the types of ships in each. Before day's end, try to launch one more attack against the enemy groups containing the most carriers.

Continue this cycle of alternating strikes and rest for your squadrons throughout the scenario, but be careful to keep your task groups from getting too close to the Japanese. Remember, as long as your planes can reach the enemy carriers and return home to their own carriers, or even conduct a strike-transfer when possible, you're close enough to the enemy. To move your task group right into the enemy's task group invites a deadly assault from the Japanese that could wipe your task group right off the map. However, by keeping your distance and gradually eating away at the Japanese carrier force with regular strikes by fresh squadrons, you'll not only be able to keep the Island of Midway safe, you'll also be able to keep the U.S. fleet intact.

10
Battlecruiser

Like Warship, Battlecruiser *is an exciting game of naval warfare that lets you control individual ships and entire divisions in battle. You'll find simulations of battles in the Atlantic from both world wars.*

★★ Jutland ★★
Death Ride of the Battlecruisers—May 31, 1916

While *Warship*'s four historical scenarios all simulate World War II sea battles in the Pacific theater, *Battlecruiser* features eight Atlantic-based ships and scenarios from both the First and Second World Wars. The inclusion of such scenarios as "Falkland Islands—December 8, 1914," and "Dogger Bank—January 24, 1915" provides players with a welcome glimpse at the naval history of a period that has been largely ignored by war game designers. In addition, the opportunity to compare the armaments and characteristics of warships from both periods gives you a sense of the gradual evolution of the modern fighting vessel.

All of *Battlecruiser*'s predesigned scenarios are played on an open sea map, although you can generate maps containing land masses for your custom-designed scenarios by using the game's built-in map-creation utility. The three basic types of scenarios are termed *battleline, transport,* and *bombardment.* In all three types of games, both players can score points by sinking or damaging enemy ships.

Scoring

The number of points you receive for each ship you sink or damage is related to the number of selection points the ship is worth. World War I battleships, for example, typically cost between 100 and 150 ship selection points (SSPs), while destroyers from the same period cost less than 10 SSPs. The huge difference in cost is because of the destroyers' lack of armor and firepower compared to the battleships. For a more detailed look at the cost of various types of ships and the features you get for your SSPs, check out the Ship Data Charts in your *Battlecruiser* manual.

In both transport and bombardment games, either the Axis player or the Allied player can also receive points when their cargo ships or warships exit off the edge of the map. The number of points awarded for each ship safely exited is identical for all cargo ships during a transport scenario. During a bombardment game, the points awarded for a safe exit of warships varies with the number and size of the ship's guns.

Division Mode vs. Ship Mode

Whether you play a battleline, a transport, or a bombardment scenario, you will control several ships that are grouped into divisions. The advantage to this grouping is that instead of having to address each ship individually, you can save time by issuing the same orders to several ships at once. Under this Division Mode, you can set the speed and the course of the entire division; order the ships within the division to open fire against the enemy with guns, torpedoes, or both; command all ships in the division to hold their fire; or change the division's formation from *line* to *parallel*, or vice versa.

In line formation, one ship is designated as the lead ship, and the other ships in the division attempt to form a line behind the leader. Although ships in line formation will automatically speed up to close gaps in the line (such as those created when ships are sunk), the speed of the division should be set within the limits of the division's slowest ship. Otherwise, some ships may be left behind.

In parallel formation, ships travel beside each other in the direction of the assigned course. Often, this type of formation allows you to bring the combined fire power of all of your division's ships against an enemy formation, or against an individual enemy ship, simultaneously. Whether to use the line or parallel formation really depends on the formation and position of the ships you're attacking. Usually, whichever formation will present the most united front against the enemy is the one to use.

Of course, there are times when you'll want to exercise even tighter control over your forces and issue specific movement and fire orders to individual ships. In the Ship Mode, which can be accessed by selecting *(E)xamine ship* from the division menu, you can adjust the course and speed of the ship currently under examination. This feature is useful for removing a severely damaged ship with a greatly reduced maximum speed from a divisional formation. If damaged ships are allowed to remain in a line formation, they may cause the ships behind them to slow down. In cases where rudder damage has caused a ship to stray off course, leaving the wounded warship in formation could result in collisions among your own ships. When a collision occurs, the damage suffered by both ships is related to the size and speed of the ships at the time of the collision.

While in the Ship Mode, you may also select specific targets for your ships by using either visual or, if available, radar fire control. This option is useful for keeping the pressure on damaged enemy ships that may still be within range of your guns, but, because of their distance from your ships, would be unlikely targets for the computer to select if left in the Division Mode. Similarly, you can aim your torpedoes manually while the Ship Mode is in effect, but unless you can easily identify the most favorable torpedo intercept angles, you'll probably have more success by letting the computer handle all torpedo launches.

British Strategy

As the Jutland II scenario begins, you are in control of 20 battleships grouped into three divisions. Each division is in line formation and has an assigned course of 180 degrees as well as an assigned speed of 15 knots. The German fleet, which also consists of 20 ships, is just off to the southwest, preparing to engage your ships in battle (Figure 10-1). Notice

Figure 10-1. Prepare for Attack

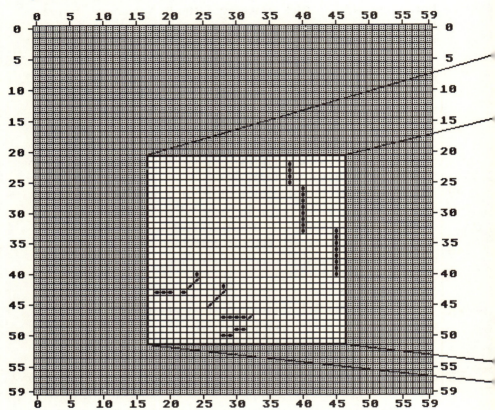

that the German task force is in four divisions. Division 1 contains four battlecruisers; Division 2 contains seven battleships; and Divisions 3 and 4 are made up of a single light cruiser and eight armorless destroyers, respectively (Table 10-1).

It may be tempting to head straight for the German destroyers in an all-out effort to rid the Atlantic of these fast, but seemingly defenseless, pests. However, there are two major problems with this approach. First, although the German destroyers have virtually no armor, they each have six 19.7-inch torpedoes that find their marks and explode often enough to make an attack with relatively slow-moving battleships fairly risky. Second, even if you do manage to hunt down and sink

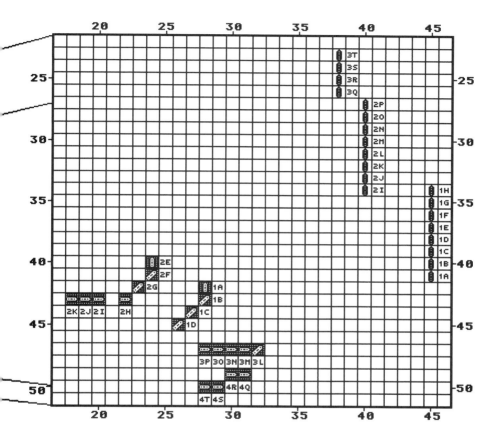

British Ships—

German Ships—

every last German destroyer, the scenario will be half over by the time you're finished, and you'll have earned less than 100 points. Remember, the points you get for sinking or damaging an enemy ship during a battleline scenario is based on the number of SSPs it costs to purchase that ship. Since World War I German destroyers usually cost less than ten SSPs each, wiping out entire divisions of destroyers isn't the quickest way to rack up the victory points.

Direct Assault

Instead, you should go right after the German battleships and battlecruisers, since each of these (with the exception of the *Von Der Tan)* is worth at least 100 SSPs. Leave your three divisions in line formation and set the course of Divisions 3 and 2 to 270 degrees, and the course of Division 1 to around 300 degrees. By assigning Division 1 a slightly northward course, you may be able to avoid becoming immediately tangled with the German destroyers. Finally, set the speed of all three divisions to 21 knots.

Although your own battleships are bound to take a lot of punishment in a direct assault against the Germans' seven battleships and four battlecruisers, because Sea Control for the scenario is Allied, the Germans will score fewer points for damaging your ships. Just remember to (E)xamine your ships and check the (D)amage display often, to monitor the fire and flood levels and possible damage to your rudder, bridge, or electrical system.

Any ships that have become severely damaged should be removed from the formation and sent to the northeast to ride out the rest of the battle in safety. As mentioned previously, you can use the Ship Mode to remove a ship from a formation. Another solution is to transfer all damaged ships to Division 9 and leave a standing order for this division to assume a parallel formation and head northeastward. Just be careful to avoid collisions among your own ships as damaged battleships scramble to get away from the action.

German Strategy

As commander of the German task force, your job is a little easier than that of your British counterpart. Although you don't have Sea Control and, consequently, won't score as many points as your opponent for damaging enemy ships, you do have a damage control rating of 4 (the best), compared to a damage control rating of just 1 (the worst), for the British fleet. This means you'll be able to control fires and repair damage easily while your opponent is plagued by spontaneous magazine explosions and similar mishaps throughout the scenario.

★★ *Battlecruiser* ★★

Table 10-1. British and German Ships

British Ships

ID	Type	Name	MG	SM	TM	Armor B	Armor D	Armor T	SP
1A	BB	*Orion*	(10)13.5/45	(16)4/50	—	12	4	11/0	21
1B	BB	*Monarch*	(10)13.5/45	(16)4/50	—	12	4	11/0	21
1C	BB	*Conqueror*	(10)13.5/45	(16)4/50	—	12	4	11/0	21
1D	BB	*Thunderer*	(10)13.5/45	(16)4/50	—	12	4	11/0	21
1E	BB	*Iron Duke*	(10)13.5/45	(12)6/45	—	12	3	11/6	21
1F	BB	*Superb*	(10)12/45	(16)4.7/45	—	10	4	11/0	21
1G	BB	*Royal Oak*	(8)15/42	(14)6/45	—	13	4	13/6	21
1H	BB	*Canada*	(10)14/50	(12)6/45	—	9	2	10/5	22
2I	BB	*Benbow*	(10)13.5/45	(12)6/45	—	12	3	11/6	21
2J	BB	*Bellerophon*	(10)12/45	(16)4.7/45	—	10	4	11/0	21
2K	BB	*Temeraire*	(10)12/45	(16)4.7/45	—	10	4	11/0	21
2L	BB	*Vanguard*	(10)12/50	(20)4/50	—	10	3	11/0	21
2M	BB	*Colossus*	(10)12/50	(16)4/50	—	11	3	11/0	21
2N	BB	*Collingwood*	(10)12/50	(20)4/50	—	10	3	11/0	21
2O	BB	*Neptune*	(10)12/50	(16)4/50	—	10	3	11/0	21
2P	BB	*St. Vincent*	(10)12/50	(20)4/50	—	10	3	11/0	21
3Q	BB	*Marlborough*	(10)13.5/45	(12)6/45	—	12	3	11/6	21
3R	BB	*Revenge*	(8)15/42	(14)6/45	—	13	4	13/6	21
3S	BB	*Hercules*	(10)12/50	(16)4/50	—	11	3	11/0	21
3T	BB	*Agincourt*	(14)12/50	(20)6/45	—	9	2	12/4	21

German Ships

ID	Type	Name	MG	SM	TM	Armor B	Armor D	Armor T	SP
1A	BC	*Derfflinger*	(8)12/50	(12)5.9/45	(8)3.5/45	12	4	11/6	25
1B	BC	*Seydlitz*	(10)11/50	(12)5.9/45	(10)3.5/45	12	4	10/6	26
1C	BC	*Moltke*	(10)11/50	(12)5.9/45	(8)3.5/45	11	3	10/6	27
1D	BC	*Von der Tann*	(0)11/45	(10)5.9/45	(12)3.5/45	10	3	9/6	25
2E	BB	*Konig*	(10)12/50	(14)5.9/45	(6)3.5/45	14	5	14/7	21
2F	BB	*Gross Kurfurst*	(10)12/50	(14)5.9/45	(6)3.5/45	14	5	14/7	21
2G	BB	*Margraf*	(10)12/50	(14)5.9/45	(6)3.5/45	14	5	14/7	17
2H	BB	*Kronprinz*	(10)12/50	(14)5.9/45	(6)3.5/45	14	5	14/7	21
2I	BB	*Kaiser*	(10)12/50	(14)5.9/45	(6)3.5/45	14	4	12/7	21
2J	BB	*Pr. Rg. Luitpold*	(10)12/50	(14)5.9/45	(6)3.5/45	14	4	12/7	21
2K	BB	*Kaiserin*	(10)12/50	(14)5.9/45	(6)3.5/45	14	4	12/7	21
3L	CL	*Regensburg*	(7)5.9/45	(2)3.5/45	(2)19.7TT	2	2	2/0	27
3M	DD	*G-41*	(3)3.5/45	(6)19.7TT	—	0	0	0/0	34
3N	DD	*V-44*	(3)4.1/45	(6)19.7TT	—	0	0	0/0	35
3O	DD	*G-87*	(3)4.1/45	(6)19.7TT	—	0	0	0/0	35
3P	DD	*G-86*	(3)3.5/45	(6)19.7TT	—	0	0	0/0	34
4Q	DD	*V-26*	(3)3.5/45	(6)19.7TT	—	0	0	0/0	34
4R	DD	*S-36*	(3)3.5/45	(6)19.7TT	—	0	0	0/0	34
4S	DD	*S-51*	(3)3.5/45	(6)19.7TT	—	0	0	0/0	34
4T	DD	*S-52*	(3)3.5/45	(6)19.7TT	—	0	0	0/0	34

Simply keeping most of your own ships in one piece until the scenario ends at 2012 won't guarantee you a victory, however. You must also aggressively attack the British battleships. Use the speed of your destroyers and battlecruisers to outmaneuver the enemy and swarm in on his wounded ships.

Head-On Against the Enemy

While your destroyers are still afloat, send Divisions 3 and 4 northward to engage the British battleships, and use your 19.7-inch torpedoes to attack the floating giants. Some of your torpedoes will be duds, and there's a good chance that all of your destroyers will hit bottom before the end of the scenario. However, because of the great difference in the SSP value between your destroyers and the enemy battleships, almost any exchange between these forces should greatly favor your side of the scoreboard. Therefore, no matter how much damage a destroyer may suffer, never take it out of action to keep it from sinking.

Once your destroyers have done their job and damaged as many of the enemy battleships as possible, send Division 1's battlecruisers in to finish off any crippled British battleships that may be heading away from the main battle area. Finally, let your battleships from Division 2 slug it out with the remaining British battleships that are still in one piece. Use the Ship Mode, when necessary, to concentrate your fire on the closest enemy ships, and never pass up the opportunity to send a damaged enemy battleship to the bottom.

11
Warship

One or two players fight it out in this tactical-level simulation of battles be-
tween Japanese and Allied navies during World War II, or you can watch
the computer take control. The scenario described here, Guadalcanal, is
one of the most remembered battles of the Pacific war.

★★ Scenario ★★
Guadalcanal I (November 13, 1942)

As the *Warship* player's manual describes, the first phase of
the Battle for Guadalcanal pitted an American force of five
cruisers and eight destroyers against a Japanese force of two
battleships, 11 destroyers, and a cruiser. In the actual battle,
the Japanese force, led by Admiral Hiroaki Abe, had a two-
fold mission: to provide cover for a convoy of transports carrying reinforcements to Guadalcanal, and to bombard the U.S.
air base at Henderson Field.

Although the scenario description in the manual states
that the Japanese lost two destroyers and a battleship (presumably the *Hiei)* in the exchange, the *Hiei,* although badly damaged, actually managed to survive the initial battle and was
later torpedoed by U.S. planes, and scuttled. The other Japanese battleship in the scenario, the *Kirishima,* also survived the
first round at Guadalcanal, but was sunk the following day by
the U.S. battleship *Washington.*

Almost half the U.S. ships involved were destroyed, but
when the battle was over, Henderson Field was left untouched
by the 14-inch guns of the *Hiei* and *Kirishima,* and seven of
the Japanese transports had been sunk by Navy and Marine
flyers. Consequently, only four Japanese transports ever
reached Tassafaronga on the northern coast of Guadalcanal,

and the 1500 men that landed did nothing to strengthen Japan's position on the island. Table 11-1 lists the ships on both sides.

Table 11-1. U.S. and Japanese Ships in the Guadalcanal Scenario

U.S. Ships

ID	Type	Name	MG	SM	TM	Armor B	Armor D	Armor T	R	SP
1A	DD	Cushing	(4)5/38	(12)15TT	-	1	0	1/0	0	36
1B	DD	Laffey	(4)5/38	(5)15TT	-	1	0	1/0	0	35
1C	DD	Sterett	(4)5/38	(16)15TT	-	1	0	1/0	0	38
1D	DD	O'Bannon	(5)5/38	(10)15TT	-	1	0	1/0	1	38
1E	CLAA	Atlanta	(16)5/38	(8)15TT	-	4	2	1/0	1	33
1F	CA	San Francisco	(9)8/55	(8)5/25	-	5	2	6/0	0	33
1G	CA	Portland	(9)8/55	(8)5/25	-	4	2	2/0	0	33
1H	CL	Helena	(15)6/47	(8)5/25	-	5	2	6/0	2	33
1I	CLAA	Juneau	(16)5/38	(8)15TT	-	4	2	1/0	1	33
1J	DD	Aaron Ward	(4)5/38	(5)15TT	-	1	0	1/0	0	35
1K	DD	Barton	(4)5/38	(5)15TT	-	1	0	1/0	0	35
1L	DD	Monssen	(4)5/38	(5)15TT	-	1	0	1/0	0	35
1M	DD	Fletcher	(5)5/38	(10)15TT	-	1	0	1/0	1	38

Japanese Ships

ID	Type	Name	MG	SM	TM	Armor B	Armor D	Armor T	R	SP
1A	BB	Hiei	(8)14/45	(16)6/50	(8)5/40	8	4	9/3	0	30
1B	BB	Kirishima	(8)14/45	(16)6/50	(8)5/40	8	4	9/3	0	30
2D	DD	Akatsuki	(6)5/50	(9)93TT	-	0	0	0/0	0	38
2E	DD	Inazuma	(6)5/50	(9)93TT	-	0	0	0/0	0	38
2F	DD	Ikazuchi	(6)5/50	(9)93TT	-	0	0	0/0	0	38
2J	DD	Asagumo	(6)5/50	(8)93TT	-	0	0	0/0	0	35
2K	DD	Murasame	(5)5/50	(8)93TT	-	0	0	0/0	0	34
2L	DD	Samidare	(5)5/50	(8)93TT	-	0	0	0/0	0	34
3C	CL	Nagara	(7)5.5/50	(8)93TT	-	2	1	0/0	0	36
3G	DD	Yukikaze	(6)5/50	(8)93TT	-	0	0	0/0	0	35
3H	DD	Amatsukaze	(6)5/50	(8)93TT	-	0	0	0/0	0	35
3I	DD	Teruzuki	(8)3.9/65	(4)93TT	-	0	0	0/0	0	33
4M	DD	Yuddachi	(5)5/50	(8)93TT	-	0	0	0/0	0	34
4N	DD	Harusame	(5)5/50	(8)93TT	-	0	0	0/0	0	34

Taking Command: Division Mode vs. Ship Mode

Warship, like many tactical combat games, lets you either select specific targets for your units or issue general commands to larger formations. If you make the latter choice, the computer handles target selection for you.

In most games that give you this choice, you're generally better off selecting targets yourself and directly controlling as much of the action as possible. With *Warship*, however, the computer actually does such a great job of target selection that you can usually hand over individual control of ships with little worry. This lets you orchestrate your attacks with much broader strokes, concentrating on overall movement and position rather than specific weapon ranges and penetration ratings.

One aspect of naval warfare that the computer handles particularly well is the launching of torpedo salvos against enemy ships. Whether because of the MK-15's lack of speed and limited range compared to the Japanese Type 93 torpedoes, or the difficulty in determining the proper angle and distance by which you should lead the enemy ships, player-directed torpedo attacks against Japanese ships are rarely successful. But, by simply using the Division mode to maneuver your ships into position, and selecting Open Fire, you'll greatly increase the number of torpedo hits against enemy ships.

Allied Strategy

Since "Guadalcanal I" is a Japanese bombardment scenario, you can safely assume that the player controlling the Japanese forces will try to move his or her two battleships off the east edge of the map. These two ships, the *Hiei* and the *Kirishima* each have eight main guns, which are worth 8 points each, or a total of 64 points per ship, if successfully exited. It's this same firepower, however, combined with the battleships' thick belt, deck, and turret armor (see Table 11-1), that makes any attempt to stop the eastward movement of these floating fortresses a little like trying to stop a pair of charging rhinos with a peashooter. Nevertheless, while it may be nearly impossible to sink either of the Japanese battleships, or even to damage them enough to stop their eastward movement, you may be able to slow them down enough to keep them on the map until the hour-long scenario ends at 2:24.

In Your Favor

One factor on your side is the vulnerability of the Japanese destroyers escorting the *Hiei* and the *Kirishima*. With virtually no belt, deck, or turret armor, the Japanese destroyers will suffer penetration and possibly flotation damage from practically any hit. Even the Japanese light cruiser, the *Nagara*, has only two inches of belt armor, one inch of deck armor, and no turret armor.

Another thing in your favor is the speed advantage your destroyers have over the Japanese battleships. Both the *Hiei* and *Kirishima* have a maximum speed of only 30 knots, while the top speeds of your destroyers range from 35 to 38 knots. However, you should set the entire division's speed to 33 knots so that you can sail northward to attack the Japanese battleships without leaving your cruisers behind.

Line Formation

At the beginning of the scenario, you'll notice that your ships are situated off the northern coast of Guadalcanal in a line, or column, formation with four destroyers at the front, the five cruisers sandwiched in the middle, and the other four destroyers pulling up the rear. Admiral Dan Callaghan, who commanded these forces at the actual battle, has, in hindsight, been criticized for leaving these ships in line formation as they sailed into battle.

Whether or not Callaghan used the right formation for the situation will never be known for sure, but, for the purposes of our simulated battle, it seems Callaghan's critics may be right. You'll find that a parallel formation that assumes a 0-degree course has the best chance of heading off the Japanese battleships and preventing them from leaving the map. By moving your ships northward until they're parallel with the *Hiei* and *Kirishima*, you force the two battleships to fight their way through the gauntlet of your entire flotilla. On the other hand, a line of ships stretched across their path is broken through as easily as the ribbon that's stretched across the finish line at the end of a marathon.

Of course there's no way to plant your ships directly in the path of the Japanese battleships without suffering a lot of damage and seeing several of your ships disappear from the map as they sink to the bottom. If you're successful in stopping the *Hiei* and *Kirishima* from leaving the map, however, it

Figure 11-1. Guadalcanal I Scenario

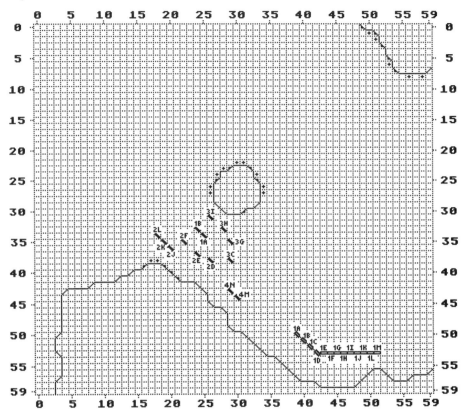

will be nearly impossible for the player commanding the Japanese forces to get the points necessary to win the scenario. Remember, in the bombardment scenario, the player trying to exit his or her ships must get twice as many points as the defending player in order to win. Figure 11-1 shows a map of the area.

Japanese Strategy

So you're stuck with 11 destroyers that don't have any armor. Look on the bright side. While they last, you've got a dozen ships (including the light cruiser *Nagara)* equipped with the best torpedoes available during the Second World War. Your Type 93 torpedoes have only a 10-percent dud rate compared to a 50-percent dud rate for the Allied MK-15s. Also, since the Type 93 warhead is more than twice the size of the MK-15's warhead, flood damage caused by torpedo hits against the Allied ships will be far greater than that caused by comparable torpedo hits against your own ships.

What's more, the speed and range of your Type 93 torpedoes blows the Allied MK-15s right out of the water. At 35 knots on the slow setting and 50 on the fast setting, the Type 93 is always a full 10 knots faster than the MK-15. In addition, with a range of 45 on the slow setting and 22 on the fast setting, the Type 93 outdistances the MK-15 by more than 3 to 1.

No Guarantees

Simply having superior torpedoes doesn't guarantee victory against the Allied Forces, however. You must also use your cruiser and destroyers to effectively keep the U.S. ships from ganging up on your battleships. This doesn't necessarily mean sending most of your destroyers to the southeast to engage the U.S. ships before they can get to your battleships. It simply means maintaining the protective formation that your ships are in at the beginning of the scenario until your small fleet is safely exited off the east edge of the map.

One of the simplest, but most effective, strategies you can use against a computer-controlled Allied force is to use the Division mode to set the course of all your ships to 90 degrees. Then, set the speed of each division to the maximum speed of the slowest ship in the division. That would be 30 knots for Division 1, 34 knots for Division 2, 33 knots for Division 3, and 34 knots for Division 4. Then wait until the U.S. ships begin firing before giving the order for your ships to fire their guns. Finally, wait an additional one or two orders phases before letting your ships open fire. This delay will insure that a large percentage of your torpedoes will find their mark.

★★ *Warship* ★★

Drawing Fire

You may notice that by following this strategy to the letter, you cause the *Teruzuki* (3I on map) to run aground on the southern coast of Savo Island. This can actually work to your advantage. As the rest of your ships are nearing the east edge of the map and are about to exit, the crippled *Teruzuki* will draw some of the Allied gunfire away from your eastbound flotilla. Of course, you can accomplish the same thing by simply using the Ship mode to set the *Teruzuki's* speed to 0 at the outset. There's also no reason why you can't simply steer this ship around the bottom of Savo Island and try to sail it off the map along with the others. Either way, if you can successfully exit both battleships and several destroyers while sinking or damaging several of the Allied ships, you'll easily earn twice as many victory points (VPs) as the Allied commander. Victory will then be yours.

12
U.S.A.A.F.

From mid-1943 until the end of the Second World War, the United States Army Air Force conducted a massive strategic bombing offensive against Axis Europe. By striking at key industries within Germany, such as steel, rubber, and ball-bearing plants, the Allies were eventually able to bring the German war machine to a grinding halt.

U.S.A.A.F. lets you simulate this two-year offensive in three phases. These phases begin on August 1, 1943; February 1, 1944; and October 1, 1944. Each phase can be played as either a one-month Short Game, or as a Campaign Game that either continues until August 1, 1945 or until industry within Axis Europe is damaged to the point that surrender is assured.

Since each game turn only represents one day of real time, a Phase 1 Campaign Game that goes the distance could take over 700 turns to complete. Fortunately, *U.S.A.A.F.* allows you to save a game in progress after three of the six phases that make up a single turn (not to be confused with the three main phases of the offensive).

The Luftwaffe Briefing

The Luftwaffe Morning Briefing is the first phase of each turn (except the first turn of the game). This briefing provides the player commanding the Luftwaffe with a detailed account of

99

the previous day's raids by U.S.A.A.F. bomber and fighter groups. The account lists the type of raids and intended targets; the number of bomber and fighter groups that participated; the number of U.S.A.A.F. bombers and fighters lost in air-to-air combat with Luftwaffe intercepters, or shot down; the number of times Luftwaffe fighter groups intercepted U.S.A.A.F. raids; and the number of Luftwaffe fighters downed in dogfights by U.S.A.A.F. fighters.

The Luftwaffe Morning Briefing also includes a weather report for the northwest, north central, northeast, southwest, south central, and southeast weather zones into which the strategy map is divided. For each of these six zones, the weather forecast is expressed as the percentage of predicted cloud cover. As you might expect, dense cloud cover reduces the odds of a successful bombing mission and increases operational losses. (You will experience fairer weather if you play the Short Game. The percentage of cloud cover during Short Game scenarios is reduced to roughly 20 percent of the cloud cover during Campaign Games.)

Also, during the Morning Briefing Phase, you can, as Luftwaffe commander, check the status of fighter groups to determine the types of aircraft available and the experience and morale ratings of the fighter groups under your command. You will find this information invaluable when you prepare for the Luftwaffe Deployment phase in which you will assign tactics to your fighters.

Defensive Strategies

Since the targets of the U.S.A.A.F. bombing raids are the various industries that keep the German war effort alive, it is important to monitor the production levels for each type of industry. During the Luftwaffe Morning Briefing, select the specific industry you wish to check. When you select electric power, for example, the computer will generate a list of all Axis cities that produce electric power, their current levels of electrical production, and the combined electrical production of all cities. In this way, you can easily determine which cities and industries have been the hardest hit by U.S.A.A.F. bombing raids. This information will help you decide where to move your airfields, fighter groups, and flak units, in order to intercept the U.S.A.A.F. bombers and their fighter escorts more effectively.

Some industries are more important than others. The most important industries are considered critical industries because other industries depend on them to maintain production levels.

The six critical industries are the ball bearings, chemicals, electric powers, railroads, steel, and rubber. Of these, electric power is the most critical because nearly all other industries run on electricity. Consider this when redeploying flak so that your most important industries will also remain the best protected.

In some cases, as commander of the Luftwaffe, you will want to replace aircraft currently in use. Although this strengthens a fighter group, bear in mind that your pilots won't be as familiar with the new aircraft types. As a result, their overall experience level could drop by as much as 50 percent. If the replacement aircraft are of the same class as those being replaced, however, there will only be a 20-percent reduction in pilot experience.

Replacement Aircraft

One of Luftwaffe commander's advantages is that he can control, to some extent, the types of aircraft that will be built in his aircraft-producing cities. Up to three different aircraft types can be built in a single city, but the total production of aircraft is limited. Therefore, a city producing one type of aircraft will be able to produce three times as many of that type, as a city producing three types.

Although the Luftwaffe commander is allowed to change the aircraft types produced by a city, any change results in a reduction in the city's overall production. For example, if you change one of the aircraft types produced in a city to an entirely different type of airplane, a 60-percent reduction in productivity occurs. On the other hand, beginning production on a new type of plane in a city previously producing only one or two aircraft types reduces overall production by 20 percent. A 20-percent drop in overall production also results when you change production of a specific aircraft type to production of a similar aircraft.

The U.S.A.A.F. Briefing

After the Luftwaffe Morning Briefing, the U.S.A.A.F. Morning Briefing phase begins. This phase is almost identical to the Luftwaffe Morning Briefing. Again, reports on the previous day's operations are available. This time, the Allied player reads the reports. It's interesting to note that on both sides, reports of enemy losses may be slightly exaggerated.

Like his or her German counterpart, the U.S.A.A.F. commander may look over the weather report and check on the status of industry production levels in Axis Europe. The U.S.A.A.F. commander can check the air groups at Allied bases in Libya, England, Italy, and Tunisia, and assign replacement aircraft where necessary. The only option open to the Luftwaffe that is unavailable to the U.S.A.A.F. is the direct control of production of various aircraft types.

Target Assignment

The third phase of each turn is the U.S.A.A.F. Target Assignment phase. During this phase the U.S.A.A.F. commander assigns raids to his various bomber and fighter squadrons.

Until the end of September 1943, raids can be launched from Allied bases in Tunisia, Libya, or England. After that date, raids can only be sent from bases in Italy or England. The Allied commander can choose among 17 targets or missions. These include raids on various industries such as chemicals, oil, steel, aviation gas, and so on, as well as military targets like U-boat, V-weapon, and air bases, and flak sites. Feint and deep-escort missions may be selected at this point.

Once a particular target or mission has been chosen, the computer will list all of the available cities that are appropriate targets. Actual target selection for flak, airfield, and feint missions is accomplished by moving the cursor to the target. A secondary target city may then be selected as long as the target type matches that of the primary target. Then, an offset point for the mission can be selected. The offset point is similar to the set-up point used in Europe Ablaze, but here your bomber and fighter groups will fly through the offset point both on their way to the target and on the return trip to their home bases.

Tactical Considerations

After the target-selection process is completed, the Allied commander must choose the bomber and fighter groups that will participate in the raid. Because of their limited speed and range, heavy bombers can't be used either to attack flak sites or to perform deep escort raids. Fighters may be used as escorts or to bomb airfields, flak sites, and railyards.

Finally, an altitude and departure time must be selected for all participating groups. During this phase, the Allied commander should use the available information screens to help guide mission strategy. The commander should examine data from previous raids, check the weather report once again, or just scan the onscreen strategy map. Once the U.S.A.A.F. commander has reviewed all available information and assigned raids to the air groups, control will shift back to the Luftwaffe commander for the Luftwaffe Deployment Phase.

The Luftwaffe Deployment

As Luftwaffe commander, you can assign five different attack strategies to your fighter groups. These are bounce attacks or direct attacks on U.S.A.A.F. fighters or bombers, and rocket attacks against bombers only.

Fighter groups assigned to bounce attack enemy fighters will only attack if they are able to gain a positional advantage over the Allied fighters. However, if your fighters are ordered to mount a direct attack on Allied fighters, they will attack even if they can't achieve any positional advantage. Since this tactic can often result in greater Luftwaffe losses, it should only be used if your situation is becoming desperate.

The direct and bounce attacks launched against Allied bombers are handled in a similar manner. The main difference is that when Allied fighters are the target of the mission and none can be found, the Luftwaffe fighters will then search for Allied bombers. If bombers are the primary target and they can't be found, your groups won't try to engage fighters. The bombers constitute the real danger. The only reason to attack Allied fighters is to neutralize them so they won't interfere with your attacks on Allied bombers.

Rocket Attack

To launch a successful rocket attack against enemy bombers, your rocket-equipped fighters must first attain the proper rocket launch position. Following the rocket attacks, your fighters will proceed to close in on the Allied bombers and pound them with cannon fire. Again, if there are no bombers in the area, your fighter groups won't waste rockets on Allied fighters.

The Combat Phase

Although tactics are assigned during the Luftwaffe Deployment Phase, specific fighter groups are assigned to intercept raids during the Combat Phase. This is done in the Luftwaffe Situation Room. This room can only be accessed by the Luftwaffe player during the Combat Phase. Here, you, as the Luftwaffe commander, can also assign fighter groups to patrol specific areas or change the locations of previously assigned patrols.

Once both players have set the forces in motion, the real action begins—not in the skies over Axis Europe, but inside your computer. Complex formulas using dozens of variables determine the results of raids, Luftwaffe fighter missions, and flak attacks. When the dust clears, you'll be informed of the aircraft losses on both sides, as well as the extent of damage to industry in Axis Europe.

13
Europe Ablaze

The air war between England and Germany in World War II brought a new dimension to traditional warfare, and with it came the need to conceptualize new tactics. Europe Ablaze *is a simulation—with three scenarios from different stages of the war—that gives a realistic view of managing this world of fighter planes, even taking into account such factors as fatigue and weather conditions.*

When the airplane was first invented, few military leaders felt it would ever have any use in warfare. However, during the First World War, the value of the airplane as a means of surveillance, and as a way of striking out at distant objectives in relative safety, began to be realized. During the Second World War, the airplane emerged as a major weapon in the arsenal of most world powers, and for nearly six years, from 1939 to 1945, the skies over Europe hummed with the sounds of bombers and fighters, recons and supply planes. The age of air warfare had arrived, and with it, a whole new field of military strategy and tactics.

Europe Ablaze simulates the air war between England and Germany, during this time, through three scenarios representative of the early, middle, and late stages of the war. These are "Their Finest Hour" (August 10–September 4, 1940), "Enemy Coast Ahead" (July 23–August 20, 1943), and "Piercing the Reich" (February 3–February 26, 1944). Figure 13-1 shows the map from the first scenario.

While employing a system of menus similar to SSG's earlier effort, *Carriers at War, Europe Ablaze* uses a two-level command structure that lets you assume the role of commander in chief, one or more of his subordinate air-fleet commanders, or both. As commander in chief, you need only issue directives to your air-fleet commanders. As air-fleet commander, you must direct the activities of the squadrons under your control according to the general strategy outlined by your commander in chief.

Figure 13-1. Their Finest Hour (Scenario 1)

Take It from the Top

If you choose to assume the role of commander in chief, you will be allowed to access the C-in-C menu once each day (at midnight) to review records, check the weather forecast, redeploy flak assets if necessary, and issue orders to your air-fleet commanders.

When you review your records, you'll be provided with information on the status of your aircraft and estimates of enemy losses, damage to friendly airfields because of enemy bombing raids, and damage to both friendly and enemy centers.

The weather report is superimposed on the strategy map and divides the map into 12 territories. Precise numeric predictions for wind speed and cloud cover are given for all friendly territories, but enemy-controlled areas are simply designated as good, fair, poor, and so forth. In addition, highlighted territories indicate the possibility of imminent storms or fog. This weather report is one of the best ways you have of determining how high to set the activity levels for your commands. Since both the weather forecast and record summary are important to the success of the next day's operations, you should consult them during each orders phase before you call up the flak adjustment or orders menu.

Flak units are made up of ground-based antiaircraft (AA) weapons that provide basic protection against assaults by enemy aircraft. Flak units are shown on the strategy map as gun icons. Select them by moving a cursor onto the unit you wish to examine. When a unit has been selected, the number of guns it contains is displayed along with the number of guns in reserve that may be allocated to existing units. Generally, the areas needing the most protection will be obvious from the locations of your major centers. As the game progresses, however, you should try to identify the primary enemy flight paths and fortify these areas.

Leadership

Now, though reading reports, checking the weather, and juggling flak units are all necessary tasks that a successful commander in chief must perform, the real reason you're in charge is so that you can tell your air-fleet commanders what needs to be done and how to do it. This includes telling each command which target types may be attacked, assigning a priority to each command for the purpose of replacement allocation, deciding how many missions each command will have available, setting the activity level of each command, and determining whether bombing attacks should be continued or aborted in the face of heavy enemy resistance. In other words, your job is to provide customized sets of parameters that your commanders must work within when they assign strike operations and patrols.

To do your job properly, you should learn as much as possible about the commands under your control. For example, before allocating missions to a command, you should check to see how many squadrons of each type of bomber, fighter, and recon plane are available. Then, keep the one-in-ten rule in mind when you hand out the missions—that is, one mission for every ten medium or heavy bomber squadrons that will be operational for the day. Also, pay careful attention to the multipliers displayed to the right of each target type. These indicate the importance your nation's supreme commander (the computer) has assigned to each of the seven target types.

Air-Fleet Command

If you decide to take on one or more of the subordinate air-fleet command positions, you'll be responsible for turning the directives of your commander in chief into specific orders for the squadrons under your command. As air-fleet commander, you'll have access to many of the same reports that your commander in chief uses, such as the records and weather summary. In addition, during the midnight and midday interphases, you'll also be allowed to assign strike operations, review the status of your squadrons, and check to see what operations have already been issued to the other (computer-controlled) commands. This will help you coordinate the overall strategy for your side.

There are four minor strike operations that you may assign to your squadrons—recon, sweep, harass, and raid. The most important air operation in the game, however, is simply called *mission*, and it consists of fighter-escorted bomber squadrons grouped together to attack facilities at a specific enemy center. The first step in directing a mission is to select a target type and an enemy center that contains that target. The target types available for most missions are population, communications, industry, and ports.

Figure 13-2. Assign Intercept Screen

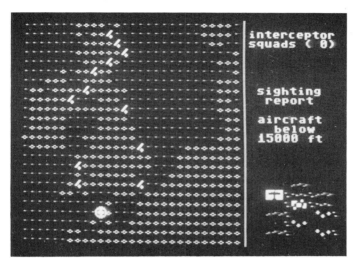

Strategy

Once the exact location of the objective is known, you must choose a centrally located set-up point where the squadrons assigned to the mission will assemble just prior to the strike. One or two "legs" may then be set for the mission. These are intermediate objectives designed to make it unclear to the ene-my's defensive forces just where you plan to attack. Although setting a second leg is often unnecessary, flying directly to the target from the set-up point will give the enemy too much warning and will decrease the likelihood of a successful attack.

Every mission that is ordered will have an estimated time of arrival (ETA). The default ETA for missions set during the midnight interphase is 1200 hours (midday), and missions or-dered during the midday interphase will have a default ETA of 0000 hours (midnight). If you wish, you can enter an ETA other than the default, but there's usually no compelling rea-son to do so.

Squadron Selection

The final steps required to set a mission are choosing the squadrons that will fly the mission, and setting the altitude at which they will cruise to the target. Squadron selection can be handled automatically by the computer, but if you insist on hand-picking the squadrons that will fly the mission, the computer will provide a list of all the squadrons that have a long enough range to reach the target and sufficient time to reach the start-up point.

If you do your own squadron selection, you should base your selections on the same criteria that the computer would use. This means you'll want to include a pathfinder squadron, all medium and heavy bombers with full payloads, and then other bombers with full payloads; and finally, any bombers with a range sufficient to reach the target, regardless of whether or not they have full payloads. Similarly, you should choose the fighters that will escort your bombers, primarily, according to their range. First, pick any fighters that can reach the target. Then, select fighters that will reach the second leg mark, the first leg mark, and finally, those that can make it to the start-up point.

For each squadron you select, you'll be required to enter an approach altitude. Here, again, the default represents the plane's optimum altitude and should usually be left unchanged. However, a higher approach altitude can sometimes take your planes out of the range of enemy AA guns. Because a higher altitude can cause your planes' flight characteristics to become unstable, attempt a high altitude approach only under good weather conditions.

Support Tactics

Although missions are your primary strike operation, it's nearly impossible to enjoy any type of overall success without supplementing your offensive effort with raids, harassments, sweeps, and, perhaps most importantly, recons. The procedure for ordering any of these operations is similar to that for a mission. The main differences among these operations are the targets that may be selected and the aircraft that are allowed to fly them.

110

A raid, for example, can be flown against any tactical targets including sea lanes, radar stations, and airfields. Raids are meant to be quick strikes that take the enemy by complete surprise; consequently, there is no set-up point or intermediate objectives. Your squadrons simply scramble, fly to the chosen target, unload their bombs, and head for home.

Harassments can be flown against any target type except population. The main difference here is that you don't select a specific target for the harassment—only the type. In other words, if you select *airfield* as the target type, throughout the day, certain squadrons will launch minor strikes against one or more computer-selected airfields. This is a great way to keep the enemy too busy to organize any major strikes against your centers while you're planning your own missions.

Defensive Measures

Of course, your enemy also has the option of launching raids and harassments against you. The best way to defend against these operations is by ordering sweeps over enemy territory. By assigning fighter and fighter-bomber squadrons to sweep operations, you may be able to intercept enemy squadrons en route to your facilities before they even get a chance to leave their own airspace.

Finally, recon-trained squadrons should be assigned to recon any enemy centers at least one day before you launch a mission against that center. This will drastically improve your chances of a successful mission by providing current intelligence on the intended target center. Like harassments, recon ops require no ETA since they are flown continuously throughout the day.

Vital Information

Besides these strike operations, which can be set only during the midnight and midday interphases, you also have access to several reports and a couple of important operations that can be ordered at any time during the day. Reports that are available throughout the day include the weather forecast and a squadron report that separates your squadrons into available, active, outgoing, returning, and stood-down categories. You can even examine squadrons individually to check their current missions and to see the number of aircraft lost or damaged. The flight paths of enemy air formations can also be checked at any time during the day to guide you when assigning patrols and intercepts.

In fact, when enemy air formations are sighted, the game will stop, and you'll be allowed to access the Assign Intercept menu. Here, you can examine the strategy map, which will now show all Axis and Allied air formations identified as either incoming or outgoing (see Figure 2). In addition, the number of aircraft in each enemy formation and their altitudes will be displayed as you cycle through them. When you spot an incoming enemy formation, don't be in too much of a hurry to send up an intercept. Allow time to click off the clock in five-minute intervals until the enemy formation is within range of your fighters. Otherwise, you'll simply exhaust your squadrons' endurance.

Other Factors

To insure that you'll always have fighters ready to intercept incoming enemy formations, set standing patrols at various times throughout the day, when enemy activity suggests that a strike against one of your centers is imminent. Don't forget, however, that all standing patrols end at midnight or midday, whichever comes first. If an enemy attack is definitely in the works, but you're not sure exactly when the strike will come, order a full patrol. This will remain in effect until the assigned squadrons have exhausted their endurance.

Fatigue is just one of several factors that help to make *Europe Ablaze* a realistic military simulation. As squadrons become fatigued, their performance is adversely affected. Eventually, a squad that is denied any R & R will automatically become unavailable because of lack of endurance. You should, therefore, try to rotate the squadrons on assignment to keep as many as possible available in case of major enemy attacks.

By taking into consideration the effects of fatigue, the influence of the weather, and the strengths and weaknesses of the squadrons under your control, you should do well commanding either side of any of the game's three scenarios.

14
Gettysburg: The Turning Point

At Gettysbury, in the rolling hills of Pennsylvania in July 1863, the fate of the Union was determined in hand-to-hand fighting. In this detailed simulation of the battle, each game turn represents one hour of realtime.

★★ Scenario: Day 1—July 1, 1863 ★★
Level: Intermediate
Difficulty level 3
No time limit, no additional cavalry reinforcements
Historical reinforcement schedule (3)
Historical ammo supply (3)

Gettysburg is considered the greatest single battle of the Civil War. It started on July 1, 1863 when the Army of Northern Virginia, led by Robert E. Lee, collided with the Union Army of the Potomac near Gettysburg, Pennsylvania. It ended two days later when a last-ditch assault by Confederate troops under the command of Major General George Pickett failed to dislodge the federal position on Cemetery Ridge. When the battle of Gettysburg was over, close to 50,000 men had died, and along with them, the Confederacy's hope of establishing an independent nation.

Union Strategy

Since the army that controls Cemetery and Culps hills at the end of the first day's fighting stands a good chance of winning the entire battle, solid control of this area is your primary goal. To win on victory points, however, you'll also have to seize and hold on to as many of the northern objectives as possible while keeping the Confederates from reaching any of theirs.

The first challenge comes from the northwest. At the beginning of the scenario, you'll find your cavalry units, Gamble and Devin, in position near Seminary Ridge along with your Cav-A artillery unit. Across the creek to the west, Heth's division sits waiting for reinforcements to pour in along Chambersburg Pike. In the south, infantry units Meredith and Cutler are located on Emmitsburg Road.

Begin by moving Devin and Gamble one square westward toward the river. Limber Cav-A artillery and move it onto the hill that's directly southwest at square (12,11). Then, unlimber the unit and change its facing back to the west. Finally, move both Meredith and Cutler northward toward Gettysburg.

As you move these units, they will be randomly assessed either zero or one fatigue point for each square they move. In general, the higher a unit's effectiveness rating, the less likely it will be charged a fatigue point for moving into a square. However, because *Gettysburg* allows you to abort any move in progress, you can always move your units as far as your operation points (OPs) will allow, without suffering any fatigue. Simply watch the fatigue display on the second screen page of unit statistics, as you move the unit. Move only three or four squares at a time, and if the unit's fatigue remains 0, quit. Then, access the unit again by pressing the space bar, and continue moving. If a unit suffers fatigue from the move, you can press Z to abort and try again.

At the first Midturn Recovery Phase, use your Cav-A artillery to bombard the nearest enemy unit. Continue to bring Meredith and Cutler northward as far as possible along Emmitsburg road, and when the I Corps artillery enters the game at square (6,51), they should also be moved northward along the same route.

Figure 14-1. The Battlefield

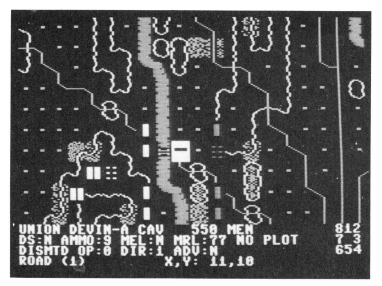

During this early stage of the battle, let Cav-A continue to fire on the closest Confederate target. Just be sure to keep an eye on their fatigue level, and rest them, when necessary, by moving them back to square (14,9). Similarly, use Devin and Gamble sparingly to avoid fatigue and casualties. When the Confederate reinforcements begin arriving from the west, you'll need all of these units in top shape.

Midmorning

By 10:00, Meredith and Cutler should be nearing the objectives at (15,13) and (15,16) on Seminary Ridge. At this point, Paul and Baxter enter the scenario at square (6,51). Like the others, these troops should be sent northward to the front.

Devin, Gamble, Meredith, Cutler, and Cav-A should all be in place by 11:00, and the I Corps should be approaching the hill at Seminary Ridge—(15,14) and (15,15). As soon as these guns are in place, assign targets for bombardment if there are any enemies within range. Other Union brigades now joining the battle include the XI Corps artillery, and the Schimmel, Krzyzan, Ames, Gilsa, Stone, and Rowley infantry units.

As you move these reinforcements toward Gettysburg, avoid stacking them atop friendly units that are in the way. This wastes operation points, since you forfeit your road bonus. To prevent this, move the units blocking the road first, even if this takes them out of the normal order of battle. At the same time, try to keep units of the same division together, even if it means not moving some units as far as their operation points allow.

As the scenario progresses and you find yourself responsible for several units scattered all over the map, two problems can develop. First, it becomes easy to overlook individual units when you're giving orders. (Remember, operation points not used aren't accumulated.) Second, as you shift units around, it becomes hard for you to keep track of which units belong together. To avoid these problems, use the N(ext) key to make sure you've issued orders to each brigade before exiting to the combat phase, and, occasionally, press I to inverse all units from the same division.

Noon

By noon, the battle really begins heating up. Coster and Smith now enter the scenario at square (21,51). Send these units north along Taneytown Road. In the north, let Gamble continue to fire at specific enemy units. The Confederates will try to flank your position by moving around to the northeast. To slow them down, use Devin to fire into squares that the Confederates might try moving into. At the same time, begin using your I Corps artillery to soften up the Confederate infantry.

If you manage to disrupt the enemy and can isolate the affected unit, try circling around with some of your own troops before you blast the enemy into oblivion. This way, if they're routed, you can capture a lot of men as they move through your zone of control while trying to get away. This is particularly useful against enemy artillery, since each captured gun is worth 100 victory points (VPs).

Continue to move the XI Corps artillery up to the front, while Cav-A bombards the enemy artillery. Bring Stone and Rowley in from the south to flank the southernmost Confederate infantry units. Keep a close watch on the fatigue levels of all your front-line troops, and as reinforcements begin arriving at the battle area, use them to replace fatigued units. In the meantime, keep Schimmel, Krzyzan, Ames, Gilsa, Coster, and Smith moving northward toward Gettysburg.

Early Afternoon

By 1:00, the main thrust of the Confederate assault becomes apparent as over 8000 Confederate troops enter the map at square (21,0). To prevent them from simply marching through Gettysburg on the way to Cemetery Hill, begin shifting your defensive position to the northeast to stretch a line of Union brigades from Mummasburg Road to Carliste Road. Schimmel, Krzyzan, Ames, Gilsa, and the XI Corps artillery should all be available by this time to help slow the Confederate movement along Carliste. Again, continue to rotate your troops to avoid fatigue while additional Union reinforcements move in from the south.

Throughout the early afternoon, keep slugging it out with the advancing Confederates. Firm up your line of defense along the northern edge of the city with the reinforcements arriving from the south. Make sure that as fresh infantry units arrive, their mode is changed from column to normal. Otherwise, their ability to fire and melee will be halved. Similarly, if you must limber artillery units to move them, you'll have to unlimber them before firing.

By the 2:00 Midturn Recovery Phase, breaks may begin to develop in the Confederate line. This is a good opportunity to try to sneak some of your own brigades through to take possession of some of the northern objectives at squares (10,1), (18,1), (21,1), (26,1), (30,1), and (34,3). At this point, a hard push to the north will weaken the Confederate assault by forcing them to divert some of their fire power to the defense of these objectives. Remember, if you can capture and maintain control of any of these squares until day's end, they'll each be worth 1000 VPs.

Midafternoon

At 3:00, Stannard enters the scenario at square (6,51) and can be sent northward along Emmitsburg Road. This is a good time to begin gradually pulling most of your forces back to protect Cemetery and Culps hills. Be careful when pulling back not to leave any disrupted units stranded among the enemy. Also, after moving a unit directly away from the enemy, remember to change its facing back to protect its flank .

Although at 4:00, additional Confederate reinforcements begin moving in along Chambersburg Pike, if you can hold them off for the rest of this turn, you'll have a good shot at keeping them off of Cemetery and Culps hills for the rest of the scenario. One reason is that, at 5:00, Ruger, McDougal, Greene, Candy, and Cobham, along with the XII Corps artillery, enter the map at square (35,35). These reinforcements can be sent directly to Cemetery Hill to help maintain control.

Evening

The last group of Union reinforcements, Graham, Ward, and the III Corps, arrive at 6:00 and enter the map at square (6,51). Because this scenario ends with the 7:00 turn, these units will never reach the battle zone and, thus, can't affect the outcome of the scenario. Fortunately, six Confederate brigades arriving at the same time at square (0,5) won't have an impact either. If you have solid control of Cemetery and Culps hills this late in the day, and if you haven't made any major mistakes like letting your artillery units retreat through enemy lines, then you can look forward, at the least, to a minor victory. Limited visibility (60 percent) during the 7:00 turn prevents many units from firing, and it's unlikely that any important objectives will change hands.

Confederate Strategy

Although the Battle of Gettysburg can't be won without gaining control of the objectives at (20,21) and (24,21)—Cemetery and Culps hills—the Confederate player who blindly charges in could end up accomplishing nothing. A far better approach is to establish intermediate and secondary goals that give you the best chances of seizing Cemetery Ridge on the first day, and at the least, prevent the Union player from winning on points.

With this in mind, you should first use your forces to drive the Union troops eastward, away from MacPherson and Seminary ridges. This lets your infantry establish a solid foothold at the junction of Chambersburg Pike and Hagerstown-Fairfield Road. This is also an excellent base of operations for an artillery assault on Cemetery Hill. Second, use your reinforcements entering from the north at 1:00 to insure that Union forces never reach any of their northern objectives.

Midmorning

Until 1:00, however, you shouldn't try anything too heroic. This means spending a good part of the morning cautiously defending the ground between Herr and MacPherson ridges by consolidating Heth's Pettigrew, Davis, Archer, and Brockenborough infantry brigades around the Pegram artillery unit. When Lane, Scales, Thomas, Perrin, and McIntosh enter the scenario at 10:00, move them southeastward along Chambersburg Pike to strengthen your position before pushing eastward. Wait at least until the 11:00 Midturn Recovery Phase and the arrival at the front of the Garnett and Poague artillery brigades, however, before attempting to cross the creek.

Early Afternoon

During the early afternoon hours, use the reinforcements pouring in from the north to guard all major roads leading to Union objectives. Specifically, send Daniel, Iverson, Doles, Ramseur, O'Neil, and Carter south to the junction of Newville and Carliste Roads before spreading westward to Mummasburg. Then, at 2:00, send Hays, Smith, Gordon, Avery, and Jones down Heidlesburg Road to the bridge that's just east of Barlows Hill. From here, these units can be spread to the east to cover Hunterstown Road and York Pike. Once all of these forces are in place, you can begin a gradual push southward toward Gettysburg.

Try to coordinate the movement of these two groups so that they arrive at Gettysburg, or come within firing range of the enemy almost simultaneously. Keep the pressure on through the afternoon; use melee attacks whenever possible to disrupt some of the weaker Union brigades. If you find a seemingly impenetrable bottleneck of Union forces in and around the city, just remember that a few routed units forced to stack through friendly squares in retreat can add fatigue and, thus, bring down the morale of several units at once. Target any particularly vulnerable Union brigades on the front line, and do everything possible to make them turn on their heels and run for cover.

Late Afternoon

If one or two Union brigades slip through your defenses and head for any of their objectives, don't waste your better units chasing after them. Instead, wait until Wilcox, Wright, Mahone, Posey, and Lang arrive at 4:00; then use these forces to drive the Union troops out of position. As the afternoon wears on, if you find yourself in solid possession of most of the land north of Gettysburg, send two units from Early's division southeastward to Hanover Road and, ultimately, the objective at (34,18). If this effort is successful and there's still some time left in the scenario, you may want to try sending one of these two units further south to try to take Wolfs Hill or, possibly, the objective at (34,35) on Baltimore Pike.

Even if you can only manage to take the objective at (21,15), you can still win the scenario on victory points if you keep your casualties low and, more importantly, keep the Union bottled up to the southeast of Gettysburg.

15
Tigers in the Snow

In December 1944, German forces made their last big counteroffensive on the Western front. This simulation lets you assume the role of Allied forces or of the German counteroffensive in the Battle of the Bulge. Each turn represents one day of realtime.

★★ St. Vith: December 16–22, 1944 ★★

The major German counteroffensive in the Ardennes that lasted from December 16 until December 27, 1944, is one of the most analyzed, studied, written-about, and recreated battles in history. This struggle, which has come to be known as the Battle of the Bulge, has been dramatized in countless books and movies and has been simulated by several computer war games (see the chapter on SSG's *Battlefront*). One of the first games to focus on the Bulge, SSI's *Tigers in the Snow* remains one of the best, and if there is such a thing as a classic computer war game, *Tigers* would certainly qualify.

Tigers in the Snow uses a system of commands for combat and movement that is simple compared with the command systems used in many of SSI's later games. In fact, the rule book that accompanies the program is only four pages long. It contains none of the complicated equations for determining such things as weapon accuracy and defensive strength normally associated with SSI's military simulations. Despite the game's relative simplicity, however, several factors—for example, the effects of terrain on movement and defensive strength, the staggered arrival of reinforcements, the strength of individual units on the battlefield, the effects of weather on air power, and the German's limited fuel supply—add to the game's realism and must be taken into consideration before you can develop a successful strategy.

The *Tigers in the Snow* St. Vith scenario lets you recreate the first six days of the Battle of the Bulge on an 11 × 19 hex map. During each of the six days from December 16 to December 22, both the Allied and German players have an opportunity to move their units and attack any enemy units in adjacent hexes. Both movement and combat are affected by a number of factors, including the combat state and supply levels of the units involved, the weather, the amount of artillery points allocated by each side, and the combat strategies selected. In addition, the strength of each unit, as expressed in combat points, is affected by the rating selected for each side at the start of the game.

Movement
The rate at which a unit can move depends on several factors, such as the type of unit being moved, the terrain that is being moved into, and whether or not the unit is moving into or out of an enemy zone of control (ZOC). As with most games that are played on a hex map, a unit's ZOC consists of the six hexes surrounding its own.

Naturally, the rougher the terrain, the harder it is for your units to move through it and the faster your movement points are exhausted. Entering a forest hex, for example, takes three times the movement points that it takes to enter a clear hex, while entering rough or westwall hexes is only twice as costly as entering clear hexes. When crossing a river, you must pay from two to five (if Allied) or from three to seven (if German) movement points, in addition to the movement cost for the hex type you are entering.

Supplies
One of the most important factors to keep in mind when you play *Tigers in the Snow* is the supply state of your units. Your general state of supply is shown as a number of supply points provided by the computer. It is displayed on the main information menu at the beginning of the movement and combat phases. At the start of the St. Vith scenario, for example, the German player has 2685 general supply points, while the Allied player has only 1135. These general supply points are

used during combat, and the rate at which they are consumed depends on the combination of strategies used by both players. In general, the harder the fighting, the more supply points that will be used up.

Of course, in order to receive all of the available supply points, a unit's local state of supply must remain in the condition described as "supplied." The local supply state of any unit depends on its combat situation. If a unit has at least three continuous hexes in its ZOC that don't contain enemy units, then it is considered supplied and will receive all available supply points. If a unit doesn't have three continuous hexes in its ZOC without enemy units, but does have at least one adjacent friendly unit, its local supply state will be limited, and its movement and combat points will be reduced by 25 percent. Finally, units with no friendly units in adjacent hexes and without three consecutive adjacent hexes free of enemies are considered isolated and will have both movement and combat points reduced by 50 percent. In addition, isolated units are prohibited from attacking or retreating when they're attacked. As a result, they will suffer additional casualties when they're successfully attacked.

There is, however, a way for the local supply state of Allied units to be improved. During clear or scattered weather, the Allied units are eligible to be supplied by airdrop, though, unfortunately, it is the computer that randomly decides whether an airdrop is successful or not. Anytime an airdrop is successful, the Allied unit's local state of supply will improve by one level. That is, an isolated unit will receive movement and combat points at the limited level, and a limited unit will receive movement and combat points as if it were fully supplied.

Combat

When you're on the attack, you have a choice of four commitment levels or combat strategies to use in the battle about to be waged. These are major, medium, light, and recon. The greater the commitment to the attack, the greater the number of casualties you are likely to suffer during the battle, but also the greater the number of casualties you may inflict on the enemy. Similarly, as the defending player, you may elect to counterattack (the strongest response), hold your position, withdraw, or perform a delaying action. Combat strategies are selected without prior knowledge of the enemy's choice, and the results of combat depend on, among other things, the combination of strategies selected.

Artillery

During the Second World War, artillery—or "indirect"—fire was used, in many cases, before an assault by ground troops to disrupt the enemy and soften his position. While *Tigers in the Snow* includes no artillery units for either the German or Allied player, both players are given a limited number of artillery points that may be allocated before battle. When attacking, you may allocate one artillery point for each unit you use to attack. When under attack, you may allocate up to two artillery points in your own defense. Since each artillery point you allocate to a battle adds ten combat points to the strength of your units, careful use of artillery can have a dramatic effect on the outcome of some battles. Just be sure not to waste artillery points on any battle that you can win without artillery support.

Although neither player is given the option of fortifying his position in preparation for an attack, each turn that a unit remains in the same hex improves its combat state and, thus, improves its chances in battle. Moving a unit, on the other hand, causes its combat state to deteriorate rapidly. In all, there are eight combat states that can be achieved (0–7), and a unit's combat points are increased by 10 percent (to a maximum of 50 percent) for each level above 0 that that a unit has reached. Therefore, when you are controlling the Allied forces, don't feel that you must move a unit each time you get the opportunity. Reinforcements should be positioned to intercept the advancing German forces, and left to improve their combat state.

Allied Strategy

The Allied player doesn't have many opportunities to score victory points. Like the Germans, you get one point for every casualty point you inflict on the enemy. In addition, 20 VPs are awarded for each unit that can break through to the east edge of the map. However, simply matching casualties point-for-point with the Germans and getting some units on the east map edge won't result in an Allied victory. You must also stop the Germans in their tracks to prevent them from reaching the northern and western edges of the map or from moving units into Marche, Rochefort, or Bastogne.

If you are unable to prevent the Germans from breaking through to the northern or western map edges, you should still do everything possible to slow their advance. Remember, the victory points they receive for exiting units decreases with each turn, so the longer you can stall them, the lower their final score. If you can, try to isolate any German unit that breaks through your line of defense by closing in on it from all sides. In this way, several weak units can gang up on a stronger German unit and eliminate it before it can reach any objective hexes or the north and west map edges.

German Strategy

One of the problems that you will have when controlling the German forces is a limited fuel supply that can slow the movement of your mechanized units. Although the consumption of fuel during movement and combat is unavoidable, you can conserve some fuel by carefully monitoring your fuel levels and avoiding any unnecessary movement. You should, therefore, take the most direct routes possible to reach your objectives and battle your way through enemy units rather than trying to go around them.

Keep in mind your primary objective of exiting as many of your strongest units as possible from the west and north map edges. The total number of points you'll receive for this depends on two variables—the combat strength of the units exited and the turn on which they leave the map. The stronger the unit and the earlier it leaves, the more points you'll receive. That's why it is important to take the initiative early, when the Allied player is weakest, and gain as much ground as you can before Allied reinforcements begin showing up.

Your secondary objective is to move in units to take the cities of Bastogne, Marche, and Rochefort. For each turn that you have a unit in position at Bastogne, you will receive 100 victory points. Rochefort and Marche are each worth only half as much, but taking control of all three early in the scenario can make the difference between a marginal or operational victory, and a strategic victory.

16
Battlefront

The fighting around Bastogne in the last days of 1944 gave new hope to Allied forces. Your job as corps commander is to marshal your troops to the best advantage. Battlefront *also includes three other World War II land battle scenarios.*

★★ Scenario ★★
Bastogne, December 18–26, 1944

In mid-December 1944, the Germans launched a desperate counteroffensive against the Allied forces in Belgium. This struggle centered on the city of Bastogne, an important crossroads that was successfully defended by the 101st U.S. Airborne Division, December 19–27. Finally, the Third Army, led by General George S. Patton, broke through to relieve the battered regiments defending Bastogne and, thus, began to turn the tide of battle in favor of the Allies. By January 29, 1945, the Allies had pushed the Germans back out of Belgium and were advancing toward the Rhine.

Bastogne is just one of four World War II land battles that you can reenact with SSG's *Battlefront*. Whether you choose to command the Allied or Axis forces, the key to winning is basically the same—gain or maintain control of the city of Bastogne and defend the position until the end of the scenario. An Allied win on victory points is possible even without maintaining control of Bastogne until the end of the scenario. However, you must keep the Germans from gaining a solid foothold in this region.

Terrain and Mobility

Like most simulations, *Battlefront* is played on a field of hexagons representing various types of terrain. A hex's terrain affects both the movement of forces through it and the success of offensives launched against it. In addition, the movement of a mechanized unit is affected differently from that of a nonmechanized unit, and the combat effect for a single type of terrain is adjusted for infantry, artillery, and armoured units. As a result, nonmechanized units can often move with relative ease through areas that are impassable to mechanized units, and an infantry battalion can sometimes assault rugged terrain more effectively than either armoured or artillery battalions.

Battlefront differs from some simulations, however, in that it doesn't let the player control the hex-by-hex movement of each battalion. Instead, orders are issued on a regimental level, and the movement of the regiment's component battalions is controlled by the computer. When advancing toward an objective, for example, you simply select the objective, and the computer will determine the best route for the battalions to take. When a contacted regiment is ordered to defend its position, battalions from the regiment that aren't within two hexes of an enemy unit automatically deploy to the most easily defended terrain in the vicinity.

While this slightly diminishes the importance of knowing the specific effects of each terrain type, it's still a good idea to study a scenario's map card before you play to familiarize yourself with the types of terrain you'll encounter. In most cases, a terrain's movement and combat effects will be obvious. Heavy woods and jungle are difficult to assault, while beach and cultivated land pose almost no resistance. Movement is easiest along roads, nearly impossible over mountains, and so on. If you're uncertain about the effects a certain type of terrain will have on movement or combat, the best way to find out is to use *Battlefront's* Creation utility to examine the scenario's terrain.

Terrain is only one of a number of variables affecting movement. How quickly you advance through specific hexes also depends on whether the adjacent hexes are under friendly or enemy control and on the number of movement points that were assigned to the advancing battalion when it was first created. Again, this information, as well as information on each battalion's equipment, strength, and range, can be gathered by using the Creation utility to examine the scenario. Cheating? No way. Just think of it as intelligence gathering.

Intelligence

There's also a wealth of useful information available during game play if you remember occasionally to check your reports before issuing orders. The first choice on the Reports menu, *Status*, shows on a single screen the condition of every battalion in the selected division. Most of this information is also available while you're issuing orders, so you don't need to check the status report very often. You will want to examine all of your divisions when you start, however, to determine at what point in the scenario each regiment becomes available to join the action. Knowing when to expect reinforcements can help you decide whether or not to hang tough in a desperate situation.

The other report that you should check out before issuing a single order is the *Objective* report. This tells you four things you'll need to know in order to win:

- The hexes that are important for you to control (objectives).
- The turns during which each of these objectives is active.
- The number of points you receive for control of these objectives during each active turn.
- The number of points you receive for control of these objectives at the end of the game.

You should also try to learn as much about the opponent's forces and objectives as you do your own. This will allow you to anticipate the movement of his forces and effectively counter his actions. Thus, you'll be able to keep his victory point totals down while boosting your own.

The Broad View

Unfortunately, all the information in the world won't do you any good if you don't know how to use the available forces effectively to achieve your military goals. Although it sounds obvious, knowing and understanding all of your options in a given situation is one of the most important factors in establishing an effective command. This means you're aware of much more than just the fact that a regiment is engaged in battle—you know you can defend, delay, launch one of four types of attacks, or place the regiment in reserve. It means knowing the probable outcome of each of these actions based on the experience level, fatigue, supply state, and casualty level of the battalions involved.

At first, it might seem that you'll need a second computer just to keep track of all the variables that can effect the outcome of battle. With experience, however, you'll learn quickly to assess any situation, and you'll know when to give up territory to save a regiment from a devastating rout, and when to launch a major offensive that will force the enemy out of an important objective.

Allied Strategy

Because of the uncertain weather and, thus, the unreliability of your air support, as well as other random factors built into the game, there's no magic formula that will guarantee an Allied victory when you're playing against the computer. Human opponents are even less predictable, but if you understand what both sides must accomplish in order to secure a victory, you'll have a good idea what your opponent is planning.

Realizing how important control of Bastogne is for both sides, you may be tempted to advance all available forces toward this objective at the start of the game in the hopes that you'll be able to hold on through all of the scenario's 31 turns. This would be a little like a football coach trying to defend against the blitz by having all of his linebackers surround the quarterback as soon as the ball is snapped. A far more effective opening strategy is to meet the Germans head-on as they enter the map from the east (Figure 16-1).

This means deploying at least one or both of the two regiments from the 1st Infantry Division in the area of Oberwampach as a delaying tactic to give the 101st Airborne Division time to reach Bastogne from the west. You should try

Figure 16-1. Bastogne Map

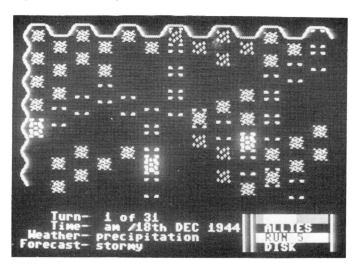

to keep the Germans occupied for at least a day and half since the 101st doesn't even enter the map until the morning of the second day. You might also consider using one of the 1st Infantry's regiments to defend the town of Noville for a while since it's active and will provide 10 victory points for the controlling player on each of the first eight turns (see Table 16-1).

By the ninth turn, all German forces will have entered and will probably have control of Oberwampach. Since all German objectives are active throughout the scenario, every turn that you control an objective takes points away from the Germans, whether or not it's worth points to you.

Win Some, Lose Some

To minimize losses, take a hard-line defensive stand only while your forces are healthy and supply is good. Otherwise, you should delay when in an engaged combat state, even if it means giving up a little ground. Once elements of the 101st Airborne begin reaching Bastogne, you can let the regiments and divisional assets from the 1st ease up a bit, especially if they've taken considerable losses. Remember, sometimes it's better to let the enemy gain ground than to let your forces get

Table 16-1. Military Objectives for Bastogne Scenario

Objective	Active Turns	Pts/Turn	Pts/End Game
Allied			
Bastogne	21–31	5	75
South Edge	23–31	5	25
Oberwampach	9–31	10	100
Longchamps	15–31	5	25
Sibret	25–31	2	10
Noville	1–8	10	0
Neffe	19–31	3	25
Hompre	15–31	2	25
Axis			
Noville	1–31	4	20
Sibret	1–31	5	25
Bastogne	1–31	10	100
Hompre	1–31	2	50
South Edge	1–31	5	150
Nives	1–31	10	50
Chenogne	1–31	10	50
Salle	1–31	10	50
Longchamps	1–31	5	25

so run down that they're useless for the rest of the game.

How well you use the forces that are defending Bastogne between your tenth and twentieth turns could determine the outcome of the game. Try to maintain a fairly wide front so that Bastogne is not simply the point on an arrow of defense. This will keep the Germans from using their 26th Infantry Division, and mechanized units of the 2nd Panzer division from encircling Bastogne from the north or south. Since the powerful U.S. 4th Armoured Division begins pouring onto the map from the south on the nineteenth turn, you may want to concentrate most of the 101st Airborne north of the river.

Once the 4th Armoured Division arrives (Figure 16-2), look for every opportunity to attack the German forces that have infiltrated the south. You'll have no trouble maintaining control of South Edge, and you may even be able to get close to Neffe if you can eliminate, or render ineffective, a few of

Figure 16-2. Arrival of the 4th Armoured

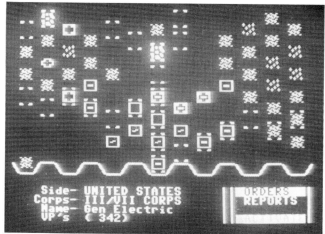

the German battalions. As it gets closer to the end of the scenario, you should become more aggressive. It's do-or-die time, so don't be afraid to pull out all the stops for the last couple of turns.

Axis Strategy

Even though the scenario begins with the Allies controlling practically the entire map, you still have a few things going for you. First, your Panzer divisions are capable of wearing down the Allied resistance around Oberwampach if you just keep the pressure on for a couple of days. Secondly, almost all of your forces are on the map by the ninth turn, while the Allies have to wait until the nineteenth turn before all three of their divisions arrive. Also, the 101st Airborne Division enters the map from the west and has farther to come to reach Bastogne. Finally, any objective you can get your hands on will begin paying off in victory points immediately, while most Allied controlled objectives aren't worth any points to them until at least the middle of the game.

To benefit from any of this, however, you must be ready to take advantage of any Allied mistakes immediately. If Allied battalions defend too aggressively too soon, you should be able to clobber them with limited probe attacks and assaults. Once you sense that the Allied forces are in trouble, go right after the vulnerable areas with exploit attacks. This will cause serious losses to the Allied regiments and could even result in elimination of some of their divisional assets, such as the 811th Armoured or 58th Artillery battalions. Just be careful not to overextend your forces since you begin the scenario with an interrupted line of sight to your divisional headquarters.

Use the time between turns 9 and 19 to really apply the pressure. This is when you'll have the Allies outnumbered, and you can use the manpower advantage to push the Allies westward and work your way into some of the central objectives in the north and south. If you can surround Bastogne by the time the last battalion of the 4th Armoured Division reaches the map on the nineteenth turn, you may be able to take control of the city before the Germans have a chance to stop you.

17
Conflict in Vietnam

Designed with historical accuracy and realism in mind, this simulation gives you an opportunity to understand some of the problems of American fighting forces in the jungles and rice paddies of Vietnam.

★★ Scenario: The Battle for Quang Tri ★★ (Variant 1, Blitzkrieg) March 30–April 6, 1972

In the spring of 1972, America's involvement in southeast Asia was coming to an end. American troop levels, once numbering over 500,000, were now down to only 150,000. For those who remained, morale was at an all-time low. It was the monsoon season and a perfect time for the opportunistic North Vietnamese Army (NVA) forces to expand their control across the demilitarized zone (DMZ) and to destroy, once and for all, the remaining pockets of the Army of the Republic of Vietnam (ARVN) resistance in the south. The NVA hoped to destabilize the Thieu regime and gain as much ground as possible before a truce.

Backed by Soviet tanks and heavy artillery, the North Vietnamese launched the largest Communist offensive since Khe Sanh. After three days of artillery and rocket bombardment, the North Vietnamese managed to push across the Cua Viet River and were advancing on Quang Tri City and Hue. The South Vietnamese offered little resistance, and it wasn't until the weather cleared and U.S. and ARVN air strikes resumed that the North Vietnamese offensive into Quang Tri Province began to slacken.

The Battle for Quang Tri City is *Conflict in Vietnam*'s fifth and final scenario. Like the others, it was designed to be historically accurate rather than simply to be a balanced contest. Thus, it decidedly favors the NVA player. It matches a powerful, Russian-backed North Vietnamese Army against ineffective and indifferent South Vietnamese forces that can hold little territory without U.S. air support. By commanding the South Vietnamese (and other) forces in this scenario, you'll understand some of the problems that faced American forces in Vietnam, and you'll have a chance to hold the ground that the South Vietnamese generals let slip away. Before you take command, however, you should understand how *Conflict In Vietnam* differs from other war games you may have played.

A Different Game

Most war games operate in *phases*. For example, many of the SSI games have a movement phase, followed by a combat phase, followed by a reinforcement phase, and finally a victory determination (or status) phase. By dividing each battle into a series of related but separate phases, the designers let you study each situation in depth and then make strategic decisions without the distraction of heavy artillery pounding down around your troops. This is necessary in most cases because, if the action were constantly unfolding, the game would be impossible to play, especially when two human players square off against one another.

Microprose's *Conflict in Vietnam* operates in what's termed *accelerated realtime*. Here, time is always ticking away (except when you're at the Orders menu, or the F key is pressed to freeze the clock). Surprisingly, in the solitaire game, once you've carefully studied the opening situation with the action frozen, the rest of the game can usually be played out in realtime with few interruptions. The resulting contest is a little like a chess game in which players aren't required to take turns, and in some ways, the constant passage of time adds to the game's realism. After all, except during an occasional cease-fire, the generals who commanded in Vietnam, or in any war for that matter, had to make strategic decisions as the battles raged.

Another problem facing American leaders in Vietnam was the difficulty in finding the enemy and fixing his position. To simulate this, *Conflict's* designers have made most of the French, U.S., and ARVN units visible to both sides throughout the game, while most of the Communist forces remain hidden until they are either spotted or contacted by free-world troops. This uncertainty about the enemy's position, combined with continuously unfolding action and appropriate delays between the issuing of orders and their execution, makes it entirely possible to launch an attack against a hex that's empty by the time the first shots are fired. If the hex is an important enemy objective, however, you can be sure there'll be somebody home when your artillery knocks on the door.

Conflict in Vietnam also differs from other war games in the flexibility with which it allows you to direct the movement of your troops. While some games give you little control over the specific hexes your battalions will defend or travel through when trying to take an objective, and others require you to direct every move your forces make, *Conflict* lets you exert as much or as little control over movement as you want. You may specify the objective hexes that your forces will move to, attack, defend, or even go to when placed in reserve. Or, if you feel confident in the unit commander's strategic abilities, you also have the option of leaving a battalion under "local command."

Because *Conflict* is played in realtime and combat situations often change rapidly with enemy movement, it's sometimes a good idea to leave certain battalions under local command. This way, even if you're busy issuing orders in another part of the battlefield, the unit's commander can react quickly in a critical situation. Since the commanding generals are usually fairly aggressive in their tactics, however, you may want to check a unit's experience and effectiveness ratings before handing over control.

Usually, though, you'll want to run the show as much as possible. When a unit is advancing toward a distant objective, for instance, it should be taken out of local command and given a number of intermediate objectives. This will insure that it takes the best route to the final destination. Also, when there are a number of possible targets within an artillery battalion's range, you'll want to decide for yourself which enemy position poses the greatest threat.

ARVN Strategy

Although the map in your game manual shows five critical objectives for the Quang Tri scenario, and a check of your onscreen reports will turn up only four, there are actually only three objectives that must be strenuously defended in order to win. If you can maintain control of Cam Lo, Dong Ha, and Firebase (FSB) Tango, the North Vietnamese will never get near Trieu Phong or Quang Tri.

As the scenario begins, there is a complete ARVN advantage. Battalions of the 2nd and 57th Infantry Regiments are in position between the NVA sanctuary in the north and the Cua Viet River. Even though it appears that these units could be stronger in a solid defensive line, a look at the underlying terrain (by pressing T) shows that many of these infantry battalions are already at forts and other strong defensive positions.

Figure 17-1. Quang Tri Scenario—Three Main Defenses

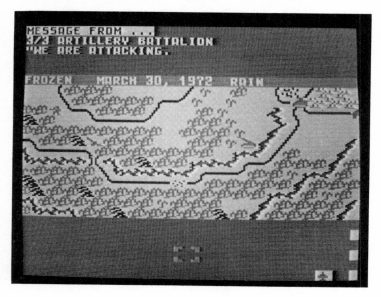

In addition, most are in fortified formation, which gives them the best chances of surviving the initial NVA onslaught.

Although constant artillery bombardment from the north will eventually force you to give up these positions, you should defend them as hard as you can for as long as you can. Then, when these units start retreating, you can try to form a solid line through the jungle and rice paddies north of the river. With the support of battalions from the 3rd Artillery Regiment positioned at firebases Beta, Gamma, and Tango, the 2nd and 57th Infantry Regiments should be able to keep the NVA infantry occupied until additional assistance arrives from the south.

The Western Front and the South

On the western front, three battalions of the 56th Infantry Regiment are defending the area from Cay Muen to just south of the fort at Khe Gio; behind them, battalions of the 147th Marine Regiment are in position at Camp Carroll and Mai Loc. These units are also in fortified formation and should be allowed to hold their ground. They're supported by the 2/I Artillery Battalion at Firebase Sarge. Additional artillery support in the west is provided by the 4th Battalion of the 3rd Artillery Regiment at Firebase Holcomb. Fortunately, the NVA forces attacking from the west aren't nearly as formidable as those along the DMZ, and the ARVN units in this area can usually hold their own with little air support.

Other ARVN units on the map, as the scenario begins, include Ruff/Puff battalions on the road south of Cam Lo and at Luong Kim, as well as armored regiments at Cam Lo and Mai Linh. The unit at Cam Lo should dig in, but it's a good idea to send the 20th Armored Battalion from Mai Linh up the road to lend support near Tango. Similarly, if the 17th Armored Cavalry Regiment shows up near Quang Tri at midnight on the first day, it should be deployed to the area of Dong Ha.

Finally, as the ARVN/U.S. commander, two of your most valuable assets will be the 41st Fighter Squadron based in the U.S. sanctuary along the south edge of the map, and the 2/I Artillery Battalion at Firebase Pedro. Both can be used for H &

I (Harassment and Interdiction) strikes into the North Vietnamese sanctuary, and to suppress specific NVA artillery battalions as they become visible. Other air units, the 1st and 2nd U.S. Bomber Wings, may become available on April 1. If they do, they can be used independently to hit additional targets, or in a concerted effort along with the fighter squadron to attack a single location. Used in combination, the three air units can eliminate almost any NVA unit from the map.

Reinforcements

The reinforcement schedule in your game manual shows that there's a 50-percent chance that three ARVN Marine Battalions will arrive on the beach in the northeast corner of the map on April 2. These should be used to add defensive strength to Firebase Tango. Also, from April 3 to April 5, a total of six Ranger Battalions will show up near Quang Tri. These units are best used to plug up holes in your defensive line north of the Cua Viet. Finally, on the last day of the scenario, April 6, an additional Ranger Battalion will arrive along with two Tactical Fighter Squadrons. Although these units may not be able to reach their objectives with only six hours left in the scenario, you should still deploy them as you would if the battle were to continue indefinitely. In the longer variant of this scenario, these forces will prove indispensable.

While few NVA units appear on the map when you start, you can assume from the historical background in your game manual that there are large concentrations of Communist forces hidden to the north and west. Although a quick peak from the enemy's perspective would show you the location of all the NVA battalions, the simulation is less enjoyable and loses its historical accuracy when you know the exact location of each of the enemy units.

Hiding NVA

Hidden in the Communist sanctuary to the north are several NVA artillery battalions and more than a dozen NVA infantry battalions, as well as a couple of tank regiments and mortar companies. Other NVA units are hidden along the edge of the jungle on the west side of the road that runs from Cay Muen south to Ca Lu. As the scenario progresses, many of the NVA units will become visible as they advance on important objectives and contact is made with your ARVN battalions.

One of the factors that makes this such a devastating assault on the South Vietnamese is that, for the first time, the Communist artillery is using powerful 130mm guns with an effective range of 18 miles. They can hit virtually any ARVN unit on the map, except the 2/I Artillery Battalion at Firebase Pedro. However, because this stationary battalion's 175mm heavy artillery has the longest range of any ground weapon in the scenario (26 miles), it can attack suspected Communist positions all over the map in relative safety.

NVA Strategy

The player commanding the Communist forces has a much easier job, especially when playing in an even game against a weak, computer-controlled ARVN. You begin the scenario with enough heavy artillery on the DMZ, literally, to destroy the effectiveness of almost any enemy battalion at will. What's more, through much of the scenario, you don't have to worry about U.S or ARVN air strikes because bad weather keeps the planes grounded. Even when the weather clears, it may be too late for the ARVN commander to save his battered forces in the north, and, with a little luck, you may be able to achieve an instant victory by capturing both Cam Lo and Dong Ha a day before the scheduled end of the scenario. Refer to Table 17-1 for a list of day codes.

One thing you should realize early is that your 9th and 24th Infantry Regiments attacking from the west are only there to give the ARVN commander something to think about. Even with the support of the 304th Artillery, Mortar, and Tank regiments, there's little chance that these units will be able to push very far eastward. Therefore, you should give them orders to attack the ARVN forces in the west and check on their condition occasionally, but don't spend very much time worrying about their progress.

Table 17-1. Operational Day Codes

Day	Code
Day 1	Jeb Stuart
Day 2	Le Loi
Day 3	White Wing
Day 4	Silver Bayonet
Day 5	Pegasus
Day 6	Muscatine
Day 7	Lam Son
Day 8	Mameluke Thrust
Day 9	Attleboro
Day 10	Nevada Eagle
Day 11	Macon
Day 12	Henderson Hill
Day 13	Masher
Day 14	Cedar Falls
Day 15	Starlight
Day 16	Junction City

Priorities

Instead, concentrate on pounding the ARVN positions in the north and breaking down their fortifications. At first, just begin shelling Con Thieu, Firebase Delta, and Gio Linh with all your 84th and 38th Artillery Regiments. Before long, you'll have the ARVN infantry abandoning their forts and scurrying back toward the river. Begin pounding the ARVN artillery at Gamma, Beta, and Tango. As the South Vietnamese are pushed southward, let your infantry and tank regiments advance toward the Cua Viet supported locally by your relatively mobile mortar companies. As soon as possible, order your infantry battalions to defend the vacated forts that the ARVN have left behind.

Check your artillery's attack objectives often, because the South Vietnamese units will be moving to get out of your line of fire. By April 3, you should be able to spot weaknesses in the ARVN line of defense. From here, it's simply a matter of blasting the South Vietnamese out of Cam Lo and Dong Ha, and moving your own forces through the ARVN defense before they can bring their reinforcing ranger battalions up. Although you shouldn't forget about the possibility of also seizing Firebase Tango, focus most of your effort on blasting a hole right down the middle.

18
Kampfgruppe

In 1942, the German army was pushing the Eastern Front toward Stalingrad and making a simultaneous thrust southward to the Caucasus Mountains. Despite advice to the contrary, Hitler ordered the offensive in the hopes that German troops would be able to capture the Caucasus oilfields by autumn. Kampfgruppe *is a platoon-level tactical game that puts you in the thick of battle.*

★★ Meeting Engagement ★★
East of Bryansk (July 7, 1942)

In the summer of 1942, German forces swept eastward toward Stalingrad and south toward the Caucasus Mountains. Their target was the oilfields of the Caucasus. Although the Russians were still trying to regroup after devastating losses of men and equipment to the German war machine in 1941, they managed to slow the German advance. The Germans eventually did capture some of the smaller oilfields, but they never reached the main sources located beyond the Caucasus. Ironically, one of the reasons for the failure to reach Russia's main oil supplies was Germany's own shortage of oil and gasoline.

While *Kampfgruppe*'s Bryansk scenario represents only one small battle in the Germans' 1942 offensive, it gives you a good sense of what the war on the Eastern Front was all about—powerful tanks like the Panzer IVG and Russian T-34, and the antitank weapons that were designed to destroy them.

Kampfgruppe was designed by Gary Grigsby, who also created *Warship* and *Mech Brigade* (both included in *The Electronic Battlefield*). Since both *Kampfgruppe* and *Mech Brigade* use the same basic command structure and have many strategic elements in common, you may want to read the *Mech Brigade* chapter before continuing. There, you'll find useful

145

information concerning such things as weapon selection, deployment, suppression, and kill probabilities—all apply equally to both games.

German Strategy

If you've ever compared the onscreen map of the Bryansk scenario with the one provided in the *Kampfgruppe* player's manual, you probably have noticed that the two maps display the battle area from different angles. The onscreen map has the large area of woods or forest situated in the east, while the map on page 9 of the manual shows the forest to the north. This discussion uses the onscreen map's perspective and refers to specific squares, when necessary, by their coordinates—(24,30) or (22,28). In some cases, however, rivers and cities are named as labeled in the manual.

The first pair of coordinates you should consider is (38,38). This is the center of the 19 × 19-square objective area. Unfortunately, at the start of the scenario, all your combat formations are on the western edge of the map, and the only forces in the objective area are Russian artillery and antitank units. Though you begin the scenario with 60 victory points and the Russians begin with none, if you want to be ahead at game's end, you'd better plan on destroying a few Russian T-34 tanks and moving as many of your own forces as possible into the objective area.

Easier said than done, of course, but the key is a plan that uses your Marders and Flak units to stop the Russian T-34s while your Wespe unit suppresses Russian antitank fire. This will let you sneak your halftracks (and loaded infantry units) up along the Vytebet River and into the objective area from the southwest, as your Panzer formations close in from the west and northwest. Refer to Figure 18-1.

Key to Figure 18-1. Combat Formations

German Forces	Russian Forces
A0 10 SMG (Loaded—A1)	A0 10 SMG
A1 12 Truck	A1 24 Truck
A2 6 Wespe	A2 6 82Mor
A3 4 88Flak (Loaded—A1)	A3 6 120Mor
A4 4 88Flak (Loaded—A1)	A4 6 120Mor
	A5 6 76AT (Loaded—A1)
B0 2 Marder	A6 6 76AT (Loaded—A1)
B1 4 Marder	A7 6 82Mor
B2 4 MardeR	
B3 4 Marder	0 5 SMG
	B1 24 Truck
C0 2 SMG (Loaded—C1)	B2 4 76AT
C1 12 Halftrk	B3 4 76AT
C2 30 Rifle/Grenade (Loaded—C1)	B4 4 76AT
C3 30 Rifle/Grenade (Loaded—C1)	B5 4 76AT
C4 30 Rifle/Grenade (Loaded—C1)	B6 4 76AT
C5 2 81Mor (Loaded—C1)	B7 4 76AT
C6 2 HMG (Loaded—C1)	
C7 4 SG-IIIG	C0 1 T34/76A
	C1 10 T34/76A
D0 5 PZ-IIIJ	C2 10 T34/76A
D1 7 PZ-IIF	
	D0 1 T34/76A
E0 2 PZ-IIIJ	D1 10 T34/76A
E1 5 PZ-IIIJ	D2 10 T34/76A
E2 5 PZ-IIIJ	
E3 5 PZ-IIIJ	E0 1 T34/76A
	E1 10 T34/76A
F0 2 PZ-IIIJ	E2 10 T34/76A
F1 5 PZ-IIIJ	
F2 5 PZ-IIIJ	F0 1 T34/76A
F3 5 PZ-IIIJ	F1 10 T34/76A
	F2 10 T34/76A
G0 2 PZ-IVG	
G1 4 PZ-IVG	
G2 4 PZ-IVG	
G3 4 PZ-IVG	

147

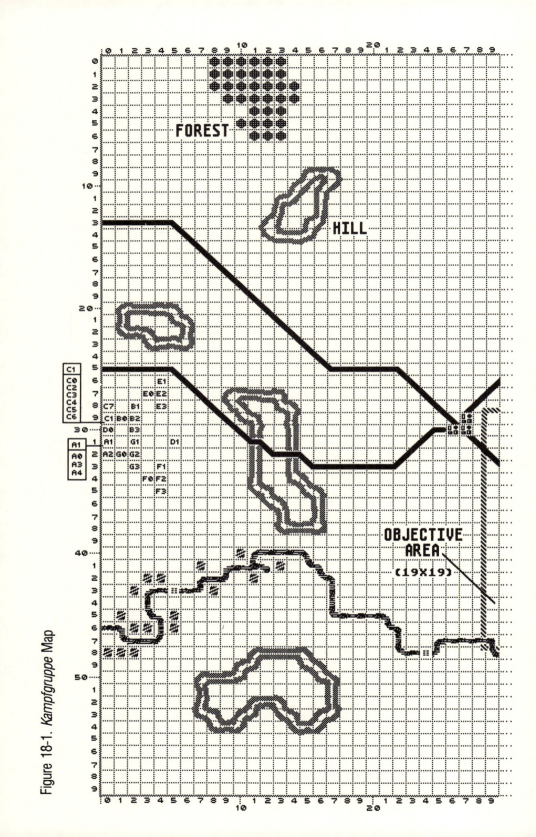

Figure 18-1. *Kampfgruppe* Map

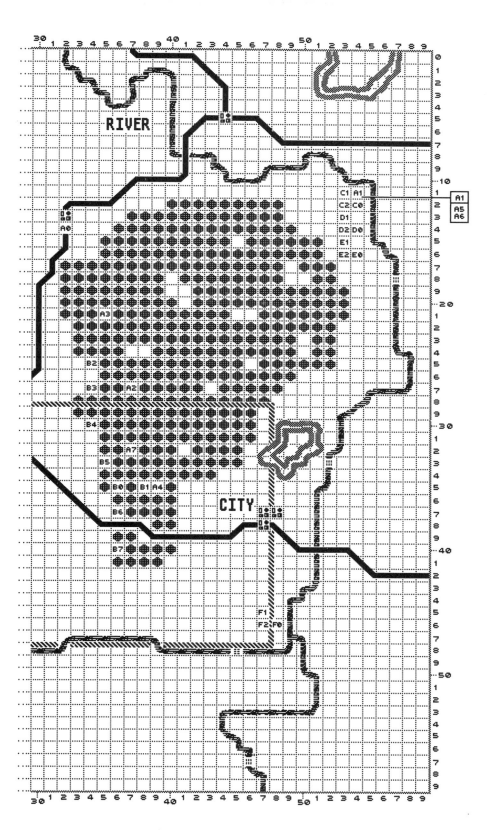

RIVER

CITY

The Push Begins

Begin by ordering your trucks (A1) to move to the large hill
that's directly east of their starting position at (0,31). Once you
have reached the hill, you can unload the two flak units (A3
and A4). Just make sure the computer-selected visibility levels
for the scenario allow an unobstructed view from your flak
units to at least column 29. This is the western edge of the objective area and the position where the Russians usually line
up their forces. If visibility is particularly poor, you'll have to
drop off your flak units closer to the front, but wherever
they're set up, don't drop them both in the same square.

At the same time, order your Wespes (A2) to move onto
the hill. Since bombardments will be called in from another
unit anyway (usually A0), it's not important that the Wespes
have an unobstructed view of the action.

Two-Pronged Assault

Next, use the *all-units* mode to move your entire Marder formation to the area around square (13,25). From here, a second
objective within the 19 × 19-square objective area can be assigned. The Panzers in your E formation should move along a
similar path just slightly ahead of your Marders.

A southern route to the objective area should also be established for formations C, F, and G. This path should take
these units south of the central hill, but north of the Vytebet
River, with the first movement objective around square
(16,39). Finally, the small D formation can be sent straight
over the hill, then on to the objective area following your two
main contingents.

One reason for splitting the attack into two separate
movement phases is to separate the two main battle groups
and, thus, to approach the objective area from two different
angles. Another is to give your units a place to stop and wait
while all of the front-line attacking forces fall into place. As
formations begin reaching their first objectives, set their
speeds to 0 until all attacking units are in place. Then, let all
units continue eastward at full speed. This way, you can develop a more unified and forceful attack.

Remember that not every unit in a formation has the same maximum speed. For example, to keep your C formation together as it moves toward an objective, let your SG-IIIGs (C7) travel at full speed, and set the halftracks that carry the rest of the formation to move at only three-quarter speed. Since the SP rating for the SG-IIIG is 12, and the halftrack's SP rating is 16, this will keep the entire formation moving together at 12.

There won't be much action for the first eight or nine turns since both you and your opponent will be jockeying for position. Once all your formations begin closing in on the objective area, though, you'll encounter antitank fire from the woods and from the first group of Russian tanks.

Fight Through

Usually, the Soviets will have only one T-34 formation in place at this point. This formation consists of a single tank as an HQ unit and two 10-tank units, which can eventually be eliminated within about three turns. Unfortunately, this is usually all the time the Russians need to move up their other three T-34 formations into place. To fight your way through the first Russian tank formation as quickly as possible, just be sure that your flak units are close enough to hit the T-34s and that your Marders arrive with your Panzers. Otherwise, the small Russian T-34 formation, along with the support of Russian antitank and artillery fire from the woods, may be powerful enough to keep you at bay until the other Russian tank units arrive. If this happens, your assault may be stopped before it starts.

Remember to unload the mortars and heavy machine guns from your halftracks as you approach the first line of Russian defense. Immediately give these unloaded units specific targets if there's anything within range, and order them to continue the advance into the objective area. When your halftracks reach the objective area, unload them right away so your infantry can use small weapons fire to suppress the T-34s. Remember, the T-34s can easily destroy all 12 of your halftracks—any infantry units left inside are instantly destroyed. Although unloaded infantry risks being overrun by the Russian T-34s, once unloaded, your infantry can use grenade attacks to defend against the Russian tanks.

As soon as most of the Russian T-34s are fully suppressed and you can spare a few Panzer units, turn your attention to any Russian 76mm antitank guns that may be firing from the western edge of the forest. These antitank units are easily destroyed, once fully suppressed, but while they last, they can thin out your Panzers and significantly slow the attack. Most important, keep the pressure on. The T-34s may seem unbeatable at first, but eventually, even these rolling fortresses will yield to a carefully orchestrated attack.

Russian Strategy

Like the player controlling the German forces, you'll have to spend the first half of the game just getting your formations into position. This means advancing your F formation westward to a point directly south of Kolosovo. Your other three tank formations, C, D, and E, must also be brought up to defend the western edge of the objective area, but how best to get them there is open to debate.

You can try the historical tactic, which was to march them around the north side of the woods and then southward to flank the German attack. Or, you can move them south along the Resseta River and then eastward to join the F formation directly.

Although either approach can be effective, the latter virtually guarantees that the majority of your forces will still be in the objective area at the end of the scenario. Whichever route your T-34s take to the front, just be sure to use the antitank and artillery units from your A and B formations to keep the Germans occupied until they arrive.

Even if you do alter history by sending your tanks to the southeast, you may still want to send your trucks (A1) along the northern route bringing with them the 76mm antitank units A5 and A6. These can be deposited somewhere in the northwest corner of the forest to broaden your front. Once unloaded, these trucks, along with your other truck unit (B1), can shuttle mortars and antitank guns around the woods to bolster your position and avoid German artillery fire.

Prepare for Attack

When your forces begin falling into place, set the ranges on most of your tanks and antitank guns on maximum, saving only HQs and a few antitank guns in reserve. The Germans have to come to you across several hundred yards of clear terrain, and if visibility is good, you'll be able to spot and possibly stop the German offensive far west of the objective area. Just remember that from their hilltop in the west, the German commanders will also have a ringside seat for the battle. If you don't suppress or eliminate them, their Wespes will be able to soften your defensive position through repeated bombardment.

19
The Ancient Art of War

Based on the writings of the Chinese philosopher Sun Tzu, The Ancient Art of War *is a war game that lets you battle it out in a variety of situations against some of the greatest military thinkers of all time. Getting inside your enemy's mind is as important as thinking out your own strategy.*

★★ Scenario: Sherwood Forest ★★
Opponent: Alexander the Great

The Ancient Art of War gives you 11 different scenarios. Possible opponents include Napoleon Bonaparte, the Greek goddess Athena, Alexander the Great, Julius Caesar, Genghis Khan, and the most formidable enemy of all, the military philosopher Sun Tzu himself. Each opponent brings his or her personal style of leadership to battle; consequently, winning often depends as much on understanding your computerized opponent's military strategy as it does on developing your own.

Athena, for example, is often so intent on capturing your flags that she pays no attention to things like the strength of your defenders, the status of her troops' food supply, or even the protection of her own flags. You can, therefore, usually defeat her by letting her charge full steam ahead at your strongest squads while you use other units to cut off her supply lines. Then, once her troops have been weakened by dwindling supplies, you can consolidate your forces and assault her flags.

Special Options

Although you have the same basic objective in each scenario, or campaign—to capture all the enemy's flags with as little direct fighting as possible— varied distribution of enemy forces over custom-designed maps gives each campaign a feel all its own. A special options menu lets you further customize campaigns by adjusting such parameters as the condition of your men, enemy visibility, and the difficulty posed by rivers, forests, and mountains. In addition, you can easily create your own original campaigns, from scratch, with the built-in game generator.

As with many war games, the battles in *The Ancient Art of War* are waged on a scrolling map of the entire battlefield. However, when opposing squads begin to mix it up, you're given the option of watching and controlling the action from an on-the-field point of view. Thus, as the struggle unfolds and casualties occur on either side, you actually see the individual soldiers fall on the battlefield. This graphic depiction of loss of life illustrates the real cost of war far better than cold statistical casualty reports provided by other war games.

Reviewing the Troops

No matter which campaign you select, you will control a number of small squads, each containing no more than 14 men. Although all squads appear identical on the war map, soldiers may be archers, barbarians, knights, or spies, or any combination of the four. Of these, the first three relate to one another in strength just as the scissors, paper, and stone do in the once-popular children's game. If you recall, the scissors cut the paper, the paper covers the stone, and the stone crushes the scissors. Similarly, the heavily armored knights fight best against the swift and agile barbarians, barbarians do extremely well against archers, and archers can use their bows and arrows to effectively combat the slow-moving knights. By keeping these relationships in mind and using the (S)ize and (I)nfo commands to check frequently the composition of enemy squads, you'll be able to avoid disastrous confrontations and take advantage of any weaknesses in your opponent's defense.

Spies are the weakest soldiers and will fare poorly in any battle. However, their ability to spot enemy movement twice as far away as other units generally protects them from attacks and makes them useful in the development of your long-range strategy. The Sherwood Forest campaign, discussed in detail later in this chapter, uses only archers, knights, and barbarians.

Whether a squad is composed of barbarians, spies, archers, knights, or some combination of the four, the formation its soldiers assume in battle is almost as important as the types of soldiers that make it up. It's usually a good idea for you to check a squad's formation before it encounters an enemy squad, to make sure that it will match up well against any enemy squads it's likely to encounter. If a squad's formation looks inappropriate for a given situation, you may select from one of nine other available formations. Five of these are standard formations that can't be altered, but the remaining four formations can be customized before you start a campaign, and they can be saved to disk.

Movement and Combat

One of the most interesting aspects of *The Ancient Art of War* is that it is virtually a phaseless war game. At any time, you can issue movement orders to any of your squads, check on the status of friendly or enemy units, or (Z)oom in on a pending encounter to give specific combat orders. However, although movement and combat continuously unfold over several areas of the map at once, only a portion of the map can be viewed onscreen at one time.

Fortunately, messages concerning enemy sightings, battle results, captured flags, and other important events that may occur beyond your view are displayed at the bottom of the screen. Pay attention to these messages and try to take care of any potentially dangerous situations before they become major problems. Remember, although your squads can move in the direction you send them and will even engage enemy squads in battle without your direction, your personal control of each encounter will help to insure a successful campaign.

Setting a Course

The Ancient Art of War movement system has an advantage over those found in games like *Field of Fire* or *Panzer Grenadier*. Instead of your simply selecting a unit and its destination, in *The Ancient Art of War* you can actually use a cursor to trace the exact path your squads will travel to reach their objectives.

Therefore, instead of having to set a number of straight-line, intermediary objectives to move a unit around an obstacle, you can simply set one course that circumnavigates the obstacle. Be careful when setting a course, however, not to let the cursor stray into rivers, mountains, or forests if you intend to keep your squad on a clear path.

Remember, also, that you can command each squad to march at either normal, slow, or fast speed. Since a fast march quickly wears down your men, you should use it only when you're trying to beat the enemy to a flag or some other key location. A normal march will also wear down your men, though not as quickly as the fast march. Finally, order a slow march when you must conserve as much of a squad's energy as possible. You may even order a squad to stop marching altogether and then restart it later without having to designate a new movement objective. While stopped at a village, a squad's condition will gradually improve until its energy is restored.

As mentioned previously, when one of your squads encounters an enemy squad, a message warns of the encounter, and you then have the option of giving specific tactical instructions to your squad in battle. After giving the general order to attack the enemy, you can instruct the entire squad, or individual sections of a mixed squad, to attack, move forward or back, or stop. If necessary, you may even direct the entire squad to retreat in an attempt to disengage from battle. Although a well-timed retreat is often the wisest choice in an impossible, no-win situation, instructing your forces to retreat is no guarantee of a clean break, and you may suffer additional casualties as your squad retreats. If it's a choice between losing a few stragglers while retreating or having your entire squad wiped out, you really have no other choice but to retreat.

Strategy and Tactics

According to the story behind the Sherwood Forest campaign, the evil sheriff (of Knottingham presumably) has raised taxes, and it's up to you and your loyal band of merry men to stand up for the rights of the villagers. This means attacking the sheriff's castle (fort) and, in doing so, driving the sheriff and his cronies out of the forest.

Since the locals are behind you on this one, the villages will supply your band with food, but the fort won't. Other rules for the game dictate that the supply line range is medium, the fort only rarely trains men, your squads start off in good condition, and the enemy is always visible. Still other rules insure that the terrain will generally be kind to your forces. Rivers, for instance, are deep but calm, and mountains are high but safe to traverse. The forests, on the other hand, are dense and may considerably slow the movement of your troops.

Beginning the Campaign

At the start of the campaign, the enemy's flag is always positioned in the heavily guarded fort on the island in the center of the map. Your own flag is in a randomly selected location chosen by the computer. Your eight squads, each consisting of six archers, are positioned in or near villages in the north and south of the battle area and in the clear to the west of the enemy's fort.

The enemy's 14 squads, consisting mainly of knights with some barbarians and a few archers thrown in for good measure, surround their fort and guard the four bridges that are the only access to the fort. Although you are outnumbered 3 to 1 (you command 48 men, while the enemy controls 140), the match-up of your archers against Alexander's knights is a favorable one and can be used to your advantage in battle. Remember, however, that fighting isn't necessarily the best way to achieve your objective. To win, you must simply locate and protect your own flag, while finding a way through the enemy's seemingly impenetrable defenses to capture his.

Capturing the Enemy's Flag

Now, although *The Ancient Art of War* strategy guide describes Alexander the Great as a leader who "will tend to protect his flag well," with a little maneuvering, you can usually get him to spread out his defenses enough to allow you to slip a squad into the fort to capture the flag. Your overall strategy, therefore, should first, be to locate and protect your own flag; then, to move squads in from the north and south to create a diversion and draw Alexander's defenders away from their fort; and finally, to sneak at least one squad in from the west to storm the fort and capture the enemy's flag.

Figure 19-1 is a map of the entire battle area showing the position of both Alexander's squads (indicated by lowercase letters) and your own (uppercase letters) at the start of the Sherwood Forest campaign. Notice that Alexander's flag is shown in the fort at the center of the map, but, because the position of your own flag varies from game to game, your flag is not shown. Usually, however, the computer will place it somewhere in the northern section of the map allowing you to protect it with squad A, B, C, or D.

Figure 19-1. Sherwood Forest

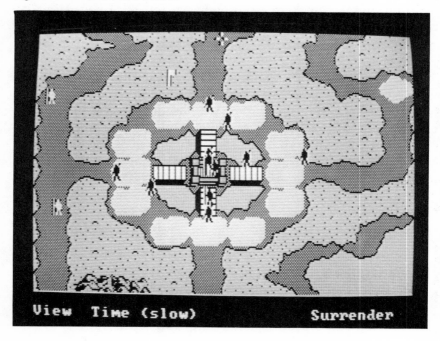

At the beginning of the campaign use the (T)ime command to set the overall speed of the game to low until you've had a chance to locate your flag and send a squad or two in to protect it. Use squads A and B if it is in the west, and squads C and D if it is in the east. The two northern squads that haven't been assigned to protect the flag can then be moved southward along one of the clear paths to try to lure Alexander's squads (a and b) away from the northern side of the fort.

Mobilization

Your next step should be to move squads G and H into the middle of the forest that's just north of the village where the two squads begin the campaign. Once in position, these two squads can simply sit and wait for Alexander's squads from the southern side of the fort to come into the forest to meet them. With any luck, squads *i* and *j*, as well as one or two squads from the eastern side of the fort, such as *f*, *g*, or *h*, will take the bait and come marching southward to attack your waiting archers.

Meanwhile, back on the western edge of the map, your own squads E and F should begin making their way off the path and into the forest areas that are just east of their starting positions. Although these units are bound to draw some attention from the few remaining forces that still guard the western side of the fort, once the enemy has been drawn out of position, either one or both of these units should be able to slip around to the vulnerable north or south sides of the fort. It may be necessary to let either E or F go to battle against Alexander's men while the other squad heads for the flag. Just be sure that once either unit makes it past the defenders, you order a fast march and stay in the clear as much as possible to give yourself the best chances of winning the foot race to the flag.

The Final Push

If there is a problem in getting either E or F into the fort, your principle alternative is to evade the enemy in the south and set either G or H up to attack the fort over the eastern or southern bridge. Again, you'll want to order a fast march and time your movement so that the enemy will get bogged down in the forest while you break into the clear and make your getaway. If you're forced to do battle with the enemy, first attack and then back off or even retreat to draw the enemy even farther away from the fort.

The only danger with this strategy is that, as you draw the enemy farther and farther away from his fort and the protection of his flag, you may actually lure him into a good position to launch a successful attack against the forces defending your own flag. After all, part of the enemy's goal is to win the campaign. If you sense that some of Alexander's squads are making a move against your flag, quickly judge whether or not you can reach his flag first. If not, you may want to pull some additional squads back to assist those units already defending your flag. If you think those squads already in position can hold their own long enough for you to get a squad into the enemy's fort, then proceed as originally planned. In either case, a persistent effort to break Alexander's defense and enter his fort will eventually reward you with victory.

20
Panzer Grenadier

You're charged with commanding an armored Panzer regiment as well as artillery battalions in this game of World War II on the Eastern Front.

★★ Scenario 1 ★★
Bridges over the Lutchessa, 1942

Like Roger Damon's other efforts—*Field of Fire, Operation Whirlwind,* and the more recent *Nam*—*Panzer Grenadier* is a tactical-level simulation that lets you command a small group of forces with a clear, short-term objective. In the Bridges over the Lutchessa scenario, for example, you command two German infantry battalions supported by assault guns, an artillery battery, and a panzer battalion. Your objective—to assault and take control of three heavily defended bridges. Victory points are awarded for every Russian tank, infantry unit, or antitank (AT) gun you destroy, and for each turn in which you have one of your own units positioned on a bridge.

Panzer Grenadier was released just one year after *Field of Fire.* Although the games are similar, *Panzer Grenadier* gives you tighter control over your forces. The main reason for this is the way in which fire and movement orders are carried out. While *Field of Fire* executes all fire and movement orders in a separate operations phase, with *Panzer Grenadier,* all orders are carried out as soon as they're issued. One of the biggest advantages of this new system is that, once an enemy unit is eliminated, you won't waste any valuable firepower by having additional units target the vacant square.

In the Trenches and On the Road

Besides greater control, *Panzer Grenadier* also offers a wider
variety of tactical options. One of these is the ability to let
your infantry, machine gun, mortar, and pioneer units dig in
to strengthen their defensive positions. This is done during the
observation phase by placing the joystick-controlled cursor
over the unit to be dug in and then pressing the firebutton.
Although units that have been dug in can still fire, they can't
be moved until they're made combat-ready again during a
subsequent observation phase.

A second tactical option lets you transport your infantry,
machine guns, mortar, and pioneer units in trucks or
halftracks. Transported units move much faster than those
afoot, of course. However, there are a couple of drawbacks.
First, you never have enough movement points to load, move,
and then unload your units in the same movement phase.
And since your units cannot fire while in transit, they have to
sit out at least one fire phase. Second, trucks and even
halftracks have little offensive or defensive strength and are
vulnerable to attack. (For a comparison of the firepower and
defensive strength of all German and Russian forces, see Table
20-1.) Despite the drawbacks, transporting your troops is the
best way to get them to a distant objective.

Table 20-1. Unit Capabilities

German Units	Firepower	Range*	Defense	Movement*
Rifle Companies	Weak	4	Good	8
Trucks and Halftracks	None	N/A	Weak	20
Machine Gun Companies	Weak	6	Good	8
Pioneers	Very good	2	Good	8
Mortar Sections	Good	25–30	Good	8
Self-Propelled Artillery	Best	Unlmtd	Fair	12
Assault Guns	Good	10	Good	16
Panzer IV	Good	10	Good	18
Panther	Excellent	12	Very good	28
Tiger	2nd Best	12	Very good	12
Russian Units	**Firepower**	**Range***	**Defense**	**Movement***
Rifle Companies	Weak	4	Good	4
T-34	Good	10	Good	18
Antitank Guns	Good	12	Good	6

* Expressed in squares

Assaults and Overruns

Another difference between *Panzer Grenadier* and its predecessor is the way assaults are made. With *Field of Fire* you were required to interrupt the operations phase by calling for a separate assault phase. With *Panzer Grenadier*, however, assaults can be carried out during any movement phase simply by moving an infantry or pioneer unit onto an enemy-occupied square. Similarly, tanks may be used to overrun enemy infantry and antitank guns.

When using either of these tactics, you should first try to soften the target with your mortars, assault guns, and even your rifles. Also, since tanks are a little tougher in this game than in *Field of Fire*, infantry assaults on enemy tanks should be avoided. Your own tanks and heavy artillery do a much better job of dealing with enemy tanks than do your foot soldiers. In general, though, whenever you can move a healthy unit onto a weaker enemy unit, you should jump at the opportunity.

Measuring Relative Strengths

One of the ways to measure the strength of enemy units is by listening and watching carefully during the enemy fire phases. Units that consistently fire three shots at your troops should be given a little extra attention, while those that are firing only once or twice can be neglected for a turn or two. This is one of the secrets to achieving a victory because it lets you keep the maximum number of enemy units suppressed with only a small group of your own forces. Just remember that, if left alone for too long, the Russian units can come back as strong as ever.

You should also carefully monitor the relative fighting strength of your own units. This is displayed in the area below the map in the form $S = 3$, where 3 is the number of subunits contained within the unit at the cursor position. Like the Russians, your own forces will gradually rebuild their strength if you give them a rest and keep them out of the line of fire for a turn or two. Remember, it's better to back off occasionally, rather than wear down your troops in an attempt to finish off the enemy all at once with assaults.

You can accidentally trigger an assault or overrun by moving into an enemy-occupied square that holds a hidden unit. When this happens, the assault or overrun is resolved in the usual way. Moving into an enemy unit by chance, however, puts you at a disadvantage because you don't get to choose where and when to assault, or which of your own units should do the assaulting. Therefore, be careful when moving weak or disrupted units through areas where the Russians might be hiding.

Overall Strategy

Since you get points for every turn in which one of your units is on a bridge, you shouldn't waste very much time in moving your infantry and machine gun units to the river. Before you load everyone into the trucks and head north, however, take a minute or two to study the map during the first observation phase. See Figure 20-1.

Figure 20-1. Bridges over the Lutchessa

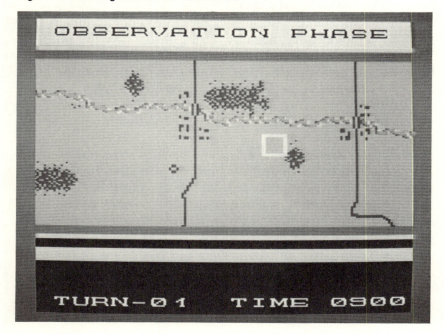

Notice the small towns surrounding each of the three bridges, the areas of forest near the central bridge, and the small hilltop just west of where the central road nears the bridge. These are the areas where the Russians will have infantry units or antitank guns waiting. Draw some of the hidden Russian units into the open by firing your mortars and artillery into the towns around the central bridge, and use your assault guns, as well as the 1st and 2nd Panzer platoons, to attack the hilltop.

As suggested in the "Scenario Tactics" section of the *Panzer Grenadier* manual, you should first concentrate on the middle and right bridges. Only when these are relatively secure should you move on the left bridge. However, instead of using all your tanks to take the middle bridge and saving your assault guns for the right bridge, as the manual recommends, you should allocate your forces in the following way.

- The infantry and heavy machine gun (HMG) units of the I Battalion should be used against the middle bridge, while the corresponding units of the II Battalion should be sent in to take the right bridge.
- The mortar sections of both battalions can remain in their starting positions throughout the scenario.
- Move your self-propelled artillery unit (SPA) onto a hilltop, out of harm's way. The SPA's unlimited range will allow it to hit any square on the map, regardless of where you put it.
- Keep both assault guns centrally located so they can quickly move in to eliminate any pockets of Russian resistance (infantry) near either bridge. Just be sure to hold them back out of the line of fire until some of the Russian antitank guns have been suppressed.

Gradually, move the 1st and 2nd platoons of your Panzer company northward to help finish off some of the AT guns. Eventually, you'll want to move these two units across the bridge on the right to flank the Russian T-34s that show up midway through the game. The third Panzer platoon can be brought northward as well; once the situation at the middle bridge appears to be under control, you should send this tank westward to take the bridge on the left.

Tactics

During the first movement phase, send all three infantry companies, and the 4th HMG Company of the I Battalion, northward along the central road until they're just east of the hilltop where the Russian infantry unit is positioned. Use these units, along with at least one assault gun and your Panzers, to force the Russian fire team down from the hilltop. Once they're in open terrain, finish them off and move one of your assault guns onto the hill to take their place. Within a couple of turns, you should try to move your infantry and MG units onto the central bridge and into the surrounding town.

Meanwhile, the three infantry companies and the 4th HMG Company of the II Battalion can be loaded into trucks and transported to the road on the right. Just be sure to cover their movement with your mortar section by shelling the Russian antitank gun in the town at the southeast corner of the right bridge.

The Central Bridge

As you gradually move your forces northward, concentrate most of your firepower on the area surrounding the central bridge. There are usually four Russian antitank guns defending this area, compared with only two at the left bridge and only one at the right bridge. These guns, along with a number of scattered infantry squads, represent the first line of Russian defense. Midway through the scenario, at least half a dozen T-34s and even more Russian infantry squads come pouring onto the map from the north to regain control of the bridges. To be ready for them, it is essential that you neutralize their first-line defenses in the early stages of the battle.

Continue to hammer at the enemy positions using your infantry, machine guns, and assault guns to silence the Russian infantry, and your mortars, artillery, and tanks to counter the enemy antitank guns. Check the underlying terrain of the enemy units during an early fire phase. Enemy antitank guns positioned in towns will be virtually impossible to eliminate without direct infantry assaults. Those in the open can be easily destroyed with a concerted effort. Wait until all of the enemy antitank guns have been weakened slightly before singling out any one for a direct assault.

The West Bridge

By the sixth turn, you should have your infantry and machine gun units in control of the middle and right bridges, and the 3rd Platoon of Panzers should be on its way westward to the left bridge. Make sure that the strongest unit of each infantry battalion is on the bridge, and that the supporting units are positioned in the surrounding towns. All of your infantry and machine gun units should be dug in, and particularly weak units should be allowed to rest whenever possible.

At this point, your 1st and 2nd Panzer Platoons should be nearing the right bridge; be ready to clear a path to let them cross the river. As soon as they've crossed, move your infantry or machine gun unit back onto the bridge and dig in once again. Then try to move these Panzers back to the west to harass the Russian T-34s. Using the cover of the forest, and with the support of your self-propelled artillery, your Panzers should be able to slow down and divide the advance of the Russian tanks.

While the major threat late in the game seems to be the Russian tanks, don't neglect the fresh infantry squads that also show up during the sixth enemy-movement phase. These should be countered with your infantry, machine guns, mortars, and assault guns. These are the two most important things to remember during the latter stages of the scenario:

- Although the shear number of enemy units that suddenly appear out of nowhere looks impossible to defend against, most of them will remain in open terrain throughout the rest of the game and will, therefore, be easy targets.
- Don't feel that you have to wipe out many of the Russian reinforcements to win. Damaging an enemy unit to the point of ineffectiveness is worth almost as much.

Using this strategy and these tactics, you should easily be able to win a major victory at the introductory level and, at least, a minor victory in the intermediate game. Be warned, however. At the advanced level, it's anyone's battle.

21
Field of Fire

Feel the heat of electronic combat in Field of Fire, *a tactical-level World War II simulation game that puts you in the shoes of an American company commander in Europe. Learn to use the tools of your trade—tanks, mortars, machine guns, and rifles—or you'll be just a statistic.*

★★ Scenario 4: Night of St. Anne ★★
June 8–9, 1944; Difficulty Level 2

It's two days after D-Day, and in the small French farming village of St. Anne, the 3rd Battalion of the U.S. 26th Infantry is trying to cut the Germans' escape route to the southeast. The Germans find themselves caught between the U.S. 1st Division closing in from the northwest and the British 2nd Army advancing from the southeast. As night falls, the Germans have realized that time is running out and that the only way to avoid getting trapped by the Allies is to break out to the south. This, however, will lead them straight through St. Anne and into a showdown with the 3rd Battalion.

The defense of St. Anne is one of eight historical scenarios that you can recreate with SSI's *Field of Fire*. Like SSI's earlier effort, *Computer Ambush,* and Avalon Hill's more recent *Under Fire, Field of Fire* is a game of tactical combat set in everyone's favorite war gaming period—World War II. What sets *Field of Fire* apart from the others is that all movement, firing, and assault orders can be issued by using joystick input. *Field of Fire* is also unique in that it lets you play a campaign game in which you battle your way through the eight scenarios. As you complete each scenario, characters that survive the fighting may be brought into the following scenario where their combat experience makes them better soldiers. The primary focus of this chapter, however, is the "Night of St. Anne."

Squad Command

Because *Field of Fire* is a tactical-level game, you're responsible for only one company of squad-sized units. Each six-man unit is represented onscreen as a single icon and is named after the squad leader. Profiles of each leader are included in the player's manual, but in combat, all units of a single type (rifle teams, for instance) seem to be created about equal.

Besides rifle teams, the game also features machine gun crews, tanks, engineers, forward observers (for calling in artillery fire), mortar crews, bazooka teams, antitank guns, and headquarters (HQ). Which types of units and how many squads of each you command depends on the scenario selected. Each type of unit has its own speed, strength, range, and so on, but you won't find elaborate tables of numeric values for any of these characteristics in the manual. Unlike the manuals that come with many of SSI's strategic war games, *Field of Fire*'s documentation uses only descriptive text to give you an overall sense of your unit's capabilities.

Similarly, the effects of various types of terrain on combat and movement aren't expressed as numeric fire modifiers, but instead are described in plain English. For example, trees are described as offering "minimal cover with little effect on movement." Hedgerows are said to present "formidable obstacles to movement." It all still comes down to number crunching inside the computer, but it seldom adds to a game when you know that a target in open terrain has a 20-percent casualty modifier and a target in town has a −10-percent casualty modifier. Doesn't it make more sense to know that you're simply safer in a building than you are on the open road?

The Tools of Combat

As you might expect, the primary fighting unit is the infantry, or rifle-fire team. In a scenario such as St. Anne, where the enemy is marching straight through town, it's important for your fire teams to occupy all the available buildings so that you can snipe at the enemy under maximum cover. Then, as you sense that enemy units have been worn down, your fire teams can move in to conduct a close assault in the open.

Other units, including your HQ, aren't able to assault enemy positions directly, so they must act in supporting roles to your infantry. Figure 21-1 gives the types of units.

Figure 21-1. Battle Units

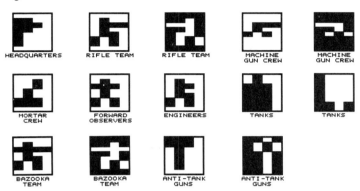

Tanks

Tanks move quickly and hit enemy targets with devastating force. However, enemy panzerfaust teams and antitank guns can easily eliminate your tanks if you use them irresponsibly. Therefore, use your tanks like highly mobile mortars until you've flushed out and destroyed any enemy antitank weapons. One way to keep your tanks safe is to push a tank close up to the front line until the enemy panzerfausts or antitank guns are spotted, and then withdraw it immediately. Then, concentrate all available fire, including your mortars, on the suspect position.

Machine Guns

A favorite *Field of Fire* weapon is the machine gun. Not only are machine guns powerful and effective over long ranges, but they sound terrific when fired. Keep your machine guns moving and ready to hammer any enemy position that becomes a serious threat. Otherwise, try to divide the available machine guns among your infantry squads. Also, in any scenario where you're trying to prevent enemy units from leaving the map, keep at least one machine gun within range of the probable exit points.

Mortars

One of the best jobs on the battlefield, at least from the soldier's point of view, is serving on the mortar crew. Because the 50mm mortars have an unlimited range, you can set them well behind the front lines and pound away at revealed or suspected enemy positions throughout the battle. Mortars, thus, have a dual purpose—to suppress known enemy positions and to perform long-distance reconnaissance by hitting possible hiding places. Of course, at these long ranges, the mortar isn't the most accurate weapon, so you should frequently reissue firing orders to your mortars.

HQ

Although your headquarters is essentially just another infantry squad and its position, relative to the other units, won't affect their performance, it's important to remember that an HQ unit may be equipped with some type of antitank weapon. This becomes a key factor late in some scenarios when the enemy tanks begin showing up. Try to keep your HQ out of trouble throughout the early stages of the game. Then, when the enemy tanks start coming out into the open, be ready to swing the HQ into action.

Taking Charge

There are only three orders you can give your soldiers—move, fire, or assault. At the beginning of the game, all your units are in the *ready* state, meaning they can accept and execute any order. However, as the battle progresses, enemy fire can cause some of your units to become *pinned* or *suppressed*. Pinned units aren't able to move, but they can fire and even assault enemy positions. They can't fire as often or assault with the strength of readied units, however.

Pinned units can become suppressed if they continue to come under attack. If this happens, the affected unit will no longer take orders and will temporarily be unable to carry out any orders already issued. Fortunately, both pinned and suppressed units can recover over time, but you should try to bring other units to their defense during this recovery period.

Movement

Although your units are usually very responsive to movement orders and will immediately begin heading for their assigned objectives, careful planning can make troop movement go much smoother. For example, avoid issuing orders that get infantry units in each other's way. When necessary, act as traffic cop by moving only a few units during each movement phase. Also, remember that if you want to move a machine gun squad or tank from one side of a building full of fire teams, diagonally, to the other side, the quickest way won't be a straight line. Instead, assign an intermediate objective that allows the unit to go around the building's perimeter.

Fire Power

Once your forces are in position and the enemy has been sighted within range, you should concentrate as much fire power as possible on each enemy position. This is the only effective way to eliminate the German units. Your fire teams can handle the German infantry squads, but more powerful enemies—such as machine guns, tanks, or panzerfausts—should be fought with units of similar strength. Particularly stubborn enemy positions should also be bombarded with your mortars.

All movement and fire orders should be checked and updated frequently. Battlefield conditions often make units lose their orders or invalidate existing orders. If an enemy moves or is eliminated, for instance, your units will continue to fire on the position until new orders are issued.

Also, remember to check the fire plot of your mortar crews frequently, since their fire can drift on its own. By maintaining tight control over all your forces, you'll give yourself the best chances of victory.

Defending St. Anne

If you look at your forces during the scenario's initial observation phase, you'll see that you have a mortar unit, an HQ, two tanks, and three eight-unit, mixed formations. Each of these mixed formations contains six fire teams, a bazooka unit, and a machine gun squad. How you distribute these forces among the surrounding buildings and hedgerows will, in large part, determine the effectiveness with which you counter the Germans' attempts to leave the map.

Start off by sending in four fire teams to occupy the two smallest buildings (A and B in Figure 21-2). Likewise, send four fire teams into Building C, six fire teams into Building D, and the four remaining fire teams into Building E.

Figure 21-2. Layout of St. Anne

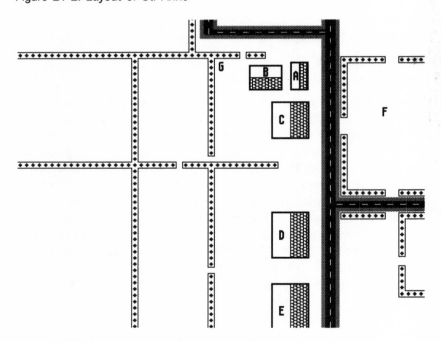

Your three machine gun units should be sent northeastward to guard the rectangular area bordered by hedgerows, designated as Area F in Figure 21-1. This is a crucial area because the Germans will either try to exit from the map here, or pass through this area on their way to the southern map edge. Either way, your machine guns are bound to see a lot of action here.

Since the German tanks must stick to the main road, you should send your three bazooka teams up the road to the intersection that's just northeast of the two small buildings. As they near the intersection, get them off the road and into the hedge-rows that line the road just to the southeast of the intersection.

Both tanks should also be sent northward along the road. The first should stop beside Building A, and the second should cut over to the west behind Building A and move into the open area to arrive, eventually, at Point G. From here, the tank will be able to fire diagonally through the break in the hedgerow to hit German tanks and infantry units that become visible along the road.

Unlike many war games in which the position and status of your HQ has a direct effect on the performance of other units, in *Field of Fire*, you don't have to worry about maintaining an unbroken line of sight to the HQ, or keeping the HQ protected behind the front lines. Bring up your headquarters into Area F to lend support to the machine guns positioned there. Although the HQ can't assault, it's very effective in suppressing and even eliminating German infantry and machine gun squads.

Finally, since your mortar crew can reach any point on the map with its 50mm tubes, leave it in its starting position. However, you may want to move it northward a few squares and onto the road, so that you won't have to scroll down as far southward every time you decide to change its fire orders. Also, if your mortars are offscreen most of the time, you may occasionally forget about them.

Fire When Ready

Once all of your units are in place, you should begin firing into areas where the Germans might be hiding. This includes hedgerows (especially along the northern edge of town, the middle of Area F, and the roads to the north). Before long, some of the German units will begin appearing. The first units to show up are usually the fire teams and machine guns. The Germans have approximately a dozen infantry squads and four machine guns. Although their primary objective is to leave the map, they'll also try to attack as many of your infantry units as possible, and suppress or destroy your bazooka teams to clear the way for their four tanks, which will soon try to make their way through town. To stifle this assault, you should attack these first German units quickly and with everything you've got.

As soon as you can determine where the heaviest fighting will be, move in the fire teams from Building D to help counter the attack. At the same time, move the fire teams from Building E straight to the east or west to a position far south of the heaviest combat. That way, if some of the Germans break through the first line of defense, you'll have forces in position to slow them down until you can move in reinforcements.

As the fighting continues, focus your gunfire on specific enemy units and move your strongest infantry squads (those *ready* units that have all six men) into adjacent squares to assault the weakened enemies. This tactic is effective against all German units, but you should avoid assaulting with pinned units or those with fewer than six men. Also, don't be afraid to assault a single German position with more than one squad at a time. If the first assault fails, the second may be able to handle the job.

Resisting the Tanks

Just when you think you've begun to get the situation under control, the German tanks will appear. Again, the best way to get rid of an enemy tank is by assaulting it from an adjacent square—the best units for the job are your bazooka teams. If all your bazookas are tied up when you need them (pinned, suppressed, out of position), a healthy infantry squad can often do the trick.

Perhaps the most important factor in battling the German tanks is to assault the first one quickly. If not, you'll soon have two to deal with, then three, and so on. This will force you to spread out your defensive fire and, as a result, you won't be able to weaken each tank effectively before assaulting. On the other hand, if you continue to try to concentrate your fire on just one tank, the others will be free to hit and suppress your units. Remember, in a close battle, your handling of the German tanks can mean the difference between a moderate victory, a minor victory, and no victory at all.

22
Combat Leader

First released in 1983, Combat Leader *is a tactical-level war game that puts you in command of tank and mechanized infantry companies in a variety of combat situations.*

Combat Leader's novice game is just that—an easily won scenario designed to let first-time players get their feet wet. When you play the novice game, you are in charge of a five-tank platoon, and your orders can be addressed either to individual tanks or to the entire platoon. You are limited, however, to instructing the tanks where to go, where to aim, and whether or not to fire.

Surprisingly, *Combat Leader*'s intermediate-level game is disproportionately complicated in comparison to the novice game. Here, you command a mechanized infantry platoon consisting of a carrier platoon and four infantry squads. Each infantry squad has its own specialized function in battle. That is, one is a security or machine gun squad, one is an antitank squad, one is a conventional rifle squad, and the last is a mortar squad. In addition to the movement and fire options available in the novice game, the intermediate game also lets you adjust the movement speed of your forces, order your mortar squad to provide a smoke screen, load your infantry into and out of their carriers, and establish patrols to flush out the enemy's position.

Although there is no advanced game, four mission games are included on the *Combat Leader* program disk. Each mission game is played on a unique battle map and has its own specific rules and victory conditions. For instance, in one scenario you're required simply to seek out and destroy as many enemy units as possible while protecting your own forces. Another requires you to take control of a specific objective and maintain possession, despite attempts by the enemy to dislodge your forces. In the third mission game, you must try to maintain a line of defense as far north as possible. The fourth puts you in command of a light armored force on a reconnaissance mission.

Taking Control

Whichever scenario you select, you'll be able to alternate between the roles of company commander and leader of any individual platoon or squad. As company commander, you may issue orders to your carrier and infantry squads, but only when you decide to step down to the level of squad leader can you control the individual carriers or infantry teams that make up your squads. When you switch from company to squad commander, the computer takes control of the squads you no longer command. However, don't expect any miracles from your computer-controlled allies. To win, you've pretty much got to keep matters in your own hands.

At various times throughout a battle, your forces will report to you concerning the completion of orders (for example, "We have dismounted"), contact with the enemy ("We are being fired on"), and the position of enemy squads that have been spotted. Intelligence reports on enemy sightings tell you which enemy platoon has been spotted, its horizontal and vertical position on the battle map, and the direction in which the platoon is traveling. It is important to pay close attention to these intelligence reports for two reasons. First, and most obvious, before you can eliminate the enemy, you have to find him and order your units to aim and fire. Second, it's often easy to lose track of which little green rectangles are your personnel carriers, and which are the enemy's. The intelligence reports help you to avoid confusing the enemy's units with your own.

Commands are issued to your forces by pressing keys. Table 22-1 lists the basic commands.

Table 22-1. *Combat Leader* Commands

Entry	Orders
C	Cease fire—don't fire until ordered (by pressing F key)
D	Dismount infantry from carrier
E	End patrol and rejoin platoon
F	Fire at will
Shift-F	All units fire
G	Go to position indicated by cursor
H	Hurry to ordered position; reduce fire
M	Mount infantry into carrier
N	Normal speed; use cover; fire if ordered and if targets are available
P	Provide patrol from your platoon
S	Supply smoke screen (available only to mortar units)
T	Target is at position marked by cursor
Delete	Use this key if you press the wrong key and want to designate another unit to receive an order

Keeping Track

Losing track of the forces under your command is a bigger problem than you might expect, and one of *Combat Leader*'s only serious flaws. The program's primitive graphics are mostly to blame. Everything on the battlefield (except the open areas) is the same shade of green. This goes for trees, depressions, tanks, rocky areas, APCs, infantry teams, and so on. In addition, all mechanized units are represented as small rectangles and, what's more, the enemy's rectangles look exactly like your own. Now picture several units from both sides charging into the woods to battle it out. Take your eyes off the action for a second and the situation becomes a hopelessly tangled mass of green.

One way to keep track of your forces on the battlefield is by designating each of the units under your control to receive an order, and then pausing for a couple of seconds to see which squares are blinking. If you're really having trouble keeping tabs on your forces after scattering them around the field, you can order them all to go to one central location to reorganize.

Know Your Battlefield

Combat Leader is played on a scrolling battle map that's one screen wide and almost three screens high (77 text lines to be exact). The area represented is roughly over 2300 meters long and 1200–1600 meters wide. Like a football field, the battle map features numbers on the sidelines to indicate your position on the field. The battlefield itself is made up of clear areas, hills, trees, depressions, and rocky areas. Each terrain type has its own effects on sighting, movement, and combat. Figure 22-1 is an example of a battle map.

Figure 22-1. Battle Map

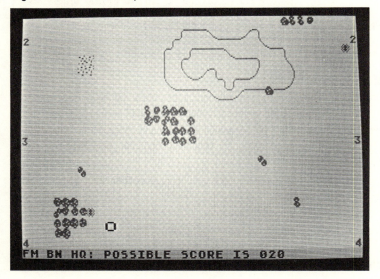

Terrain and Movement

Because *Combat Leader* is a tactical-level game, it's often helpful to picture yourself down on the battlefield while you're playing. Examine the position of the various terrain features and keep in mind how each type of terrain can affect the game. Terrain features such as trees and hills are impossible to see through in real life, so don't expect to spot enemy infantry carriers on the other side of such an obstacle unless you've got a patrol in a position with a direct line of sight to the enemy.

Avoid rocky areas since these will slow down your forces while offering little protection. For good protection against enemy fire, hide your units in depressions. Trees also offer good cover, but they restrict your visibility and prevent the units hiding in them from spotting the enemy. Depressions, on the other hand, offer good visibility. Remember, also, that no matter which type of terrain your forces occupy, they'll be able to spot enemy units only within a 90-degree arc in the direction they are looking. Therefore, until the enemy position is known, try to spread out your forces and adjust their aim to cover as much of the battlefield as possible with several overlapping arcs of visibility. Another limiting factor, with regard to sighting, is distance. Whether or not your forces have an unobstructed view, the maximum distance they can see in any direction is 24 characters.

Traditionally, hills are considered to be excellent defensive terrain, and the same holds true in *Combat Leader*. Unfortunately, because the map for the intermediate game features hills only in the northern section of the battlefield, and your forces begin in the south, the computer-controlled forces begin the game in a better position to seize control of the hills.

When you're moving forces from one section of the battlefield to another, the speed at which the units have been ordered to move will affect the path they take to reach their destination. At normal speed, your forces will stick close to available cover for protection, even if it slows them down somewhat. If ordered to hurry, your forces will pass up covering terrain in favor of clear areas to reach the objective as quickly as possible.

Tools of the Trade

Because each of the infantry squads you command has a specific duty on the battlefield, a variety of weapons are necessary to get the job done. Your rifle squad, for example, carries a light antitank weapon, such as a bazooka, in addition to its M-16s. Larger antitank weapons armed with armor-piercing shells are carried by your antitank squad. Security squads pack machine guns (MGs) capable of firing 240 rounds per minute, and your mortar squads can launch two different types of shells from their mortars—high-explosive shells for clearing out enemy infantry positions, and smoke shells that can be used to screen the movement of your forces from the enemy's field of vision.

The four carriers that make up your carrier squad also come equipped with both antitank guns and MGs to protect your infantry squads while in transit. While mounted, your infantry squads are unable to fire their own weapons.

Strategy and Tactics

When the game begins, locate your carrier platoon (D) and order it to move to the horizontal center of the map at its current vertical position. When all four infantry squads have reached this objective, order a patrol to be sent out from Platoon D. The enemy is to the north and the patrol will help your forces to locate them. While your patrol is out hunting, try to find one depression for each of your infantry squads to hide in until the enemy has been flushed out. If possible, advance your squads northward to around vertical position 45. The four depressions found here offer good visibility and protection.

Don't get too comfortable, however, because the key to winning is maintaining a very mobile and flexible team of infantry squads. As soon as the first enemy units are spotted, call off your patrol and set everyone's sights just to the south of the reported position. (The enemy will be traveling southward, and this will cause it to move into the line of fire.) Use your mortars to bury the enemy in smoke while your other units pound away with deadlier weapons. Once the enemy's glasses have been sufficiently fogged up, let your mortars unload some of their high explosive shells.

If the enemy pinpoints the location of any of your squads, order that squad to stop firing and move it immediately to an area with better cover. If an enemy unit appears damaged, order your forces to converge on it to finish it off. If not, it could recover and get back into the action. By the same token, if any of your own forces become damaged, protect them at all costs by bringing your healthy units to their aid.

At the earliest opportunity, try to drive the enemy from the hills in the northern half of the battlefield and move your own units onto them. You get no extra points for maintaining control of an objective, however, so only remain in this position as long as it gives you an edge, and your infantry squads are in no danger of being eliminated.

If you find one of your infantry squads in close contact with an enemy squad, you may want to take over as squad commander for that unit, order your fire teams to dismount from their carrier, and begin issuing orders to the individual two-man teams. While this does give you more control in a specific area, and can be effective in some circumstances, it is generally better to address each command to an entire squad. This is especially true early in the game when you still have all of your squads intact. Then, as the battle wears on and carriers, or even entire squads, are destroyed, you'll have plenty of opportunity to command on the squad level.

Despite its simple format and the general lack of mathematics in the player's manual, *Combat Leader* is not an easy game to win. Although it's very difficult to wipe out the enemy completely without losing a squad or two, a patient offense that stays in motion should be able to wear down the enemy and nail down a win for the home team.

23
Gulf Strike

Once again, the Middle East and the Persian Gulf have made the front pages. This simulation, though not an historical reenactment of recent events, gives a sense of urgency because of its closeness to the contemporary world.

Avalon Hill's *Gulf Strike* is one the most frightening of the computer war games discussed in this book, because it is the one that most closely mirrors the military events of recent history. According to the scenario description on the game box, Iranian interference in support of Afghanistan rebels has caused the June 6, 1988 assault by the U.S.S.R., against the Iranians. The justification for the Soviet attack is a 1921 Treaty of Friendship agreement giving the Soviets the right to intervene if anyone should use Iran as a base of operations for an attack on Russia.

While *Gulf Strike* teams the United States and Iran against the Soviet Union and Iraq, actual events in the Persian Gulf since the game was first released in software format, in 1986, have greatly changed the complexion of the fighting in and around the Gulf. Today, it is the Iranians who find themselves politically and diplomatically isolated from nearly all of the factions with military presence in the Persian Gulf. Although it was Iraqi fighters who launched Exocet missiles against the U.S.S. *Stark*, the Iraqis seem more willing, at this point, to sit down and come to a peaceful settlement to this on-going struggle, than do the Iranians who continue to mine the gulf, endangering military and cargo vessels alike.

The Computer Version

This simulated version focuses more on the ground war that is being waged on the land surrounding the Gulf. However, naval operations and air missions are also included to add to the game's realism. *Gulf Strike* is played on a scrolling strategic map of the Persian Gulf, which is divided into 3640 squares, each representing an area 28 × 28 kilometers. The terrain consists of ocean, mountain, desert, rivers, swamps, clear areas, and other natural elements. In addition, several artificial structures such as cities, towns, oil rigs, airbases, bridges, and seaports also dot the landscape, and some of these can affect the movement of your units.

Unlike many games that give you several scenarios from which to choose, *Gulf Strike* offers only one. It can be played by two human players or as a solo contest against the computer. If you do choose to play against the computer, however, you will have a choice of three difficulty levels—easy, medium, and hard.

Rules of the Game

Twenty-one of the map's 3640 squares are designated as Victory Point Squares. At the start of the game the U.S./Iranian forces are in control of all of them. In order to win, the player controlling the Soviet/Iraqi forces must capture nine Victory Point Squares before 25 turns have been played. Since each turn represents two days of realtime, an entire game simulates the fighting over a period of one and a half months. See Table 23-1 for the name of each Victory Point Square and its map coordinates.

Table 23-1. Victory Point Squares and Positions

Victory Point Square	Coordinates
Abadan	(14,40)
Abu Zhabi	(36,64)
Ahvaz	(15,37)
Arak	(19,26)
Bandar Abbas	(45,55)
Dubay	(39,61)
Esfahan	(27,32)

Victory Point Square	Coordinates
Hamadan	(16,22)
Kashan	(26,26)
Kerman	(48,42)
Kermanshah	(10,23)
Mashad	(56,17)
Oman Point	(43,58)
Qazyin	(22,17)
Qeys Island	(35,57)
Qom	(25,24)
Rasht	(21,13)
Shiraz	(30,44)
Tabriz	(9,9)
Tehran	(27,20)
Zanjan	(16,15)

Figure 23-1. The Persian Gulf

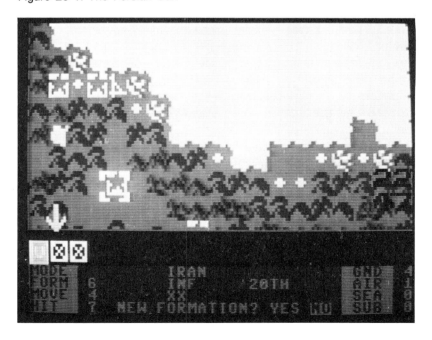

If necessary, you can save the game in progress, or you can simply end it before the 25 turns have been played out or the Soviet/Iraqi player has captured 9 Victory Point Squares. If the game is cut short in this manner, the number of enemy hit points eliminated by each side will be displayed, but neither player will have achieved a real victory. See Figure 23-1 for a map of the Gulf area.

Phases

Each two-day turn is divided into three main phases, which in turn are subdivided into several shorter phases. The first phase—the Ground Naval Movement Phase—lets the player commanding the U.S./Iranian forces change the formations of his or her ground and naval units and move them to other positions on the map that are within their movement limitations. The commander of the Soviet/Iraqi forces then gets an opportunity to do the same thing.

That phase is followed by the Air Movement and Combat Phase in which the U.S./Iranian player creates and launches air and surface strikes against Soviet/Iraqi positions around the map. The results of these strikes, along with any interception attacks by the Soviet/Iraqi forces, are resolved by the computer, and the planes flown during these missions return either to their bases of origin or to other nearby bases that you select for them. During this phase, each air squadron is eligible to fly as many as three consecutive missions, as long as there are enough active planes left in the squadron to fly. Once all of the U.S./Iranian air strikes have been completed, the Soviet/Iraqi forces get their turn.

Finally, during the Ground/Naval Combat phase, the computer automatically matches up units with enemies in adjacent squares and resolves the combat that takes place between them, taking into account the combat strengths of the units involved and the various modifiers that are in effect because of such factors as terrain and formation. As adjacent units battle it out with each other, they lose a certain number of hits each time they are damaged in combat. This number of hit points is similar to the hit points possessed by characters in fantasy/role-playing games: When a unit's HP level reaches 0, the unit has been destroyed and is consequently removed from the map.

Formations and Modes

A unit can be in six different formations, and each formation has specific effects on movement and combat. The formation that should be used for traveling is called *Travel*; although it allows your units to move faster than any other formation, it also leaves them more vulnerable to attacks by the enemy. In fact, a unit's combat strength, when it has been attacked in the Travel formation, is only one quarter of what it would normally be.

Between two defense formations and two attack formations, is a formation called *Move to Contact*. When one of your units is in the Move to Contact formation, it isn't particularly weak or strong. The two formations used for defense—the *Hasty Defense* and the *Deliberate Defense*—both improve your unit's chances in the event of an enemy attack. You can more quickly change into the Hasty Defense, although it offers less protection. You should use it when a sudden attack doesn't allow you enough time to really dig in with the Deliberate Defense.

Similarly, the *Hasty Assault* can be more easily achieved than a *Deliberate Assault*, but the combat strength of a unit performing a Hasty Assault won't be nearly as great as the combat strength of a unit that has taken the extra time to launch a Deliberate Assault. The combat strength of a unit in the Deliberate Assault formation is roughly 33 percent greater than the same unit in the Hasty Assault formation. Although combat between adjacent stacks is automatically handled by the computer during the Ground Combat Phase, only units that aren't in either type of defense formation will attack.

Movement Points

A unit's formation, while it is moving, has a big effect on the number of movement points that it will expend for entering various types of terrain. In Travel formation, for example, a unit can enter any square for only 25 percent of the cost in movement points that it would take if the unit were in Move to Contact formation. Units in Move to Contact formation simply pay the standard movement cost to enter any square. A unit in a Deliberate Assault formation, on the other hand, will pay four times the cost in movement points to enter a square as it would in Move to Contact formation. When a unit is in either the Hasty Assault or the Hasty Defense formations, the cost to enter a square is double the going rate for that type of terrain.

Notice, also, that it can cost armored units up to twice as many movement points to enter certain types of terrain as it costs for nonarmored units. Swamps and mountains, for instance, cost four movement points for nonarmored units and eight for armored units. The costs for nonarmored and armored units entering rough desert are three and six movement points, respectively. Three types of terrain are prohibited to movement by both armored and nonarmored units alike. These are impassable mountains, the ocean, and rivers. Rivers can be crossed only at bridges, and only bridges can be entered by both armored and nonarmored units for the same movement-point cost (4 MPs).

Units also use up their movement points simply by entering and exiting the various formations. As you might expect, the costliest formations to enter are the two Deliberate formations. These both cost four movement points to enter. Each of the Hasty formations costs only two movement points to enter. The others cost one movement point each. Leaving a formation is generally cheaper, costing just two movement points to leave a Deliberate Assault formation and one or no movement points to leave the others.

Modes

Just as ground units can be set in a variety of formations, air units have three different modes that are used, depending on their intended missions. In the Interception mode, an air unit will defend against enemy air attacks anywhere on the map. Since this is the only line of defense against enemy air attacks, be sure not to allocate all of your air forces to strike missions, since this will leave no one minding the fort.

Your main type of strike is the Surface Strike in which available air units are sent to attack specific enemy ground targets. To accompany and protect the air units on Surface Strike missions, you must also send some air units in the Air Strike mode to escort the squadons performing the Surface Strike. Otherwise, the enemy would be able to intercept the Surface Strike with no trouble. Whichever modes you assign to your air units, just be certain that all squadrons are given missions appropriate to the plane type they contain.

The Combatants

One of the things that adds greatly to the strategic depth of *Gulf Strike*, is the variety of unit types that are represented in the game. Over a dozen different types of forces take part in the conflict, including rangers, infantry, artillery, mechanized units, airmobile and air defense units, marine amphibious brigades, and even special forces. In addition, units range in size from individual battalions all the way up to entire divisions.

To examine any of your forces, you simply move the joystick-controlled cursor over the stack of units you wish to examine and press the firebutton. Icons representing the individual units in the stack are then displayed across the stack window below the onscreen map. An arrow is used to select the unit you wish to examine.

Battle Prep: Necessary Information

When a unit has been selected, information about the unit appears in the Status/Message Display at the bottom of the screen. Here you are told not only the nationality, type, and size of the unit, but also the unit's current formation, the number of movement and hit points it has remaining, and the unit's combat values. These four values represent the unit's strength against the four general types of forces that it may encounter in battle. These are ground forces, air forces, ships, and submarines. Studying the combat values of all of your units before moving them to within striking distance of enemy forces is one of the most important ways you can prepare for battle. By doing so, you can avoid dangerous mismatches that could result in your units getting promptly massacred.

Another useful source of information that can contribute to your success in battle is the "Ground Combat Resolution Table" on page 11 of the *Gulf Strike* instruction manual. This table presents the odds ratios and combat differentials that will be in effect, depending on the comparitive strength of the attacking and defending units. Once you've played *Gulf Strike* a number of times, however, you'll begin to sense your odds in most situations almost intuitively, and can dispense with the table and rely solely on your combat experience to guide you to victory in the Gulf.

24
Arcticfox

An alien enemy from planet STV-7X has dug into the snow of Antarctica and aims to destroy the earth's supply of oxygen—that's where the supertank code named Arcticfox *comes in.*

★★ Tournament Mode ★★
Enemy Configuration 1, Starting Location 1

During the nineteenth century, few people would have dreamed that one day we'd be waging war with heatseeking missiles, military surveillance satellites, and nuclear-powered submarines. Yet today, these weapons are considered standard equipment for the world's superpower arsenals. So although the idea of a 37-ton tank that can dig itself into and out of packed snow, and go from 0 to 144kph in about a second may seem a little farfetched, who can say what types of weapons the armies of tomorrow will be using? Chances are, research already underway by both the United States and the Soviet Union into the military uses of artificial intelligence and robotics will result in sophisticated, twenty-first-century combat vehicles that will make the Arcticfox look like some type of extinct fighting dinosaur.

One thing is pretty certain. If a tank such as the Arcticfox were to be developed, it's unlikely that it would be used against alien invaders from planet STV-7X to prevent them from converting the earth's atmosphere to some unbreathable mix of ammonia, methane, and chlorine gas. Instead, we'd probably sell these tanks to the aliens from planet STV-7X so that they could overtake the inhabitants of STV-8X and convert *their* atmosphere. Oh, well, since interplanetary arms sales aren't an option with *Arcticfox*, I guess you'll just have to battle it out.

Weapons

Named for two of its designers—Damon Slye and Richard Hicks, the Slye-Hicks MX-100, otherwise known as the Arcticfox, is equipped with two mine dispensers and carries 15 mines into battle. You can use these to shake pesky tanks and recon sleds off your tail, or you can simply unload them as a precautionary measure when you're traveling through heavily defended areas. The Fox also carries 10 optically guided missiles, each with its own remote camera to help you guide it to the target. Once a missile has been launched, you can monitor the view from the missile by using either the small Radar/Aft View screen in the center of your instrument panel, or the large main screen that usually shows the forward view from within the tank.

The Arcticfox's main weapon, however, is a 150mm cannon with a virtually unlimited supply of shells. This weapon is effective against all alien land vehicles and planes as well as air converters. Radar towers, rocket launchers, and the aliens' communications and main forts should be attacked from long range using your missiles.

Instrumentation

The Fox's one-person crew cabin is practically bare compared to the dashboards of many automobiles. Nevertheless, it does contain everything you'll need to help you locate and destroy the aliens' main fortress. The three most important instruments are those used to pinpoint your location and guide you around the frozen Antarctic wasteland that the aliens have decided to call home. These are the radar/aft view, the position indicator, and a rotary compass.

The radar/aft view actually has three functions. As a radar screen, it gives you an overhead view of the battlefield with your Arcticfox in the center, and north at the top of the screen. By comparing the radar view with the position of the rotary compass hand, you can easily steer the Arcticfox around the frozen terrain. This display can also be toggled to show the area directly behind your tank. Although the operator's manual suggests using this view to guide the placement of mines, in most cases, the radar view is adequate for this purpose.

And, as we've mentioned, the radar/aft view can also be used to view the scene from the on-board missile cameras. This not only allows you to guide missiles to their targets, but it can also give you an advance peek at areas just beyond the horizon. Just make sure you have an ample supply of missiles before allocating any to this type of reconnaissance.

Figure 24-1. Instrument Panel

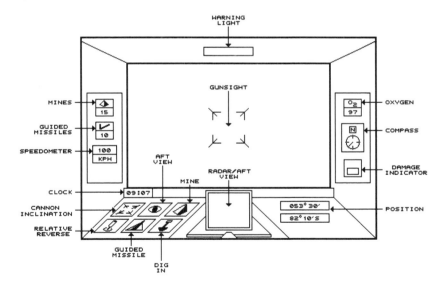

Also on the instrument panel are six icon-labeled indicators that represent six important Arcticfox functions, or systems. When the Fox's guided missiles, mines, aft view, cannon inclination mode, relative reverse, or dig-in function is in use or damaged, the corresponding indicator changes color to let you know. Other indicators along the left and right side of the cockpit show the number of mines and missiles remaining, your speed (in kilometers per hour), the amount of damage the Arcticfox has suffered, and the percent of oxygen left unconverted. Finally, there is an enemy radar warning indicator at the top of the screen; it turns from green to yellow when you've been spotted by the enemy. If the communications fort discovers your position and broadcasts it to all forces on the map, the indicator will turn red.

Figure 24-2. Icon-Controlled Systems

Function	Icon	Function	Icon
Guided Missile		Cannon Inclination	
Mine		Relative Reverse	
Aft View		Dig In	

Strategy

Because the background material in the operator's manual describes the conflict as a race to stop the aliens from converting all of the earth's oxygen, you may be tempted to cruise around knocking out every air converter you can find. While this would slow the rate of oxygen conversion, in the long run, it would also subject you to more enemy fire than would a direct assault on the main fortress. If your Arcticfox is destroyed by enemy fire, you lose no matter how many converters you've leveled.

A much better approach is simply to go in for the kill. If you're successful, you'll find that there's plenty of oxygen left for the human survivors.

Figure 24-3. Map of *Arcticfox* World

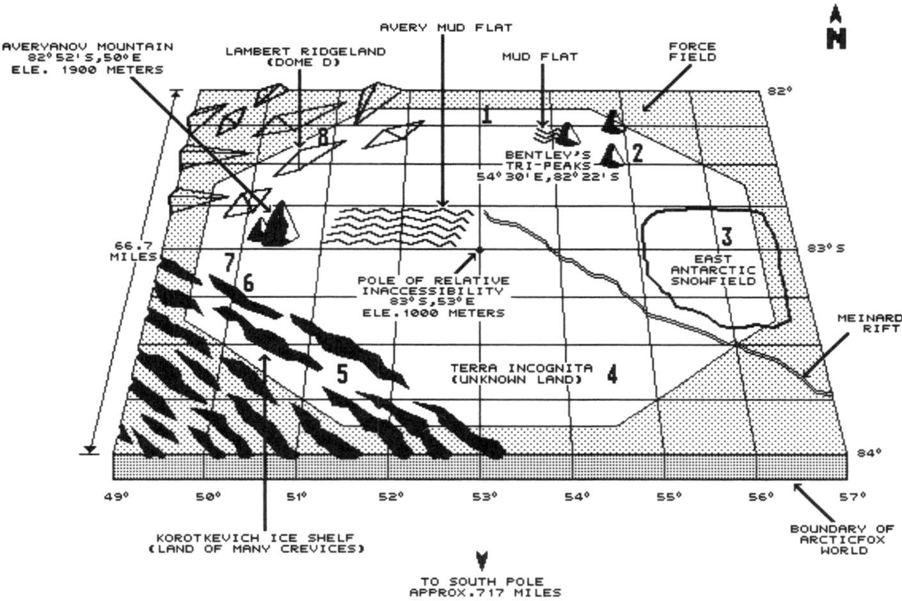

Moving Out

Since all starting locations are roughly the same distance from the aliens' main fort, it doesn't really matter which one you select. For this scenario, however, I arbitrarily selected starting location 1. This puts your Arcticfox at 53° 33'/82° 08' at the beginning of the game. If you check the map of the *Arcticfox* world in Figure 24-3, you'll see that this places you several miles north-northeast of the Pole of Relative Inaccessibility. Starting locations 2–8 follow clockwise from this point around the perimeter of the map. The specific coordinates of all eight starting locations are as follows:

(1) 53° 33'/82° 08'   (2) 55° 25'/82° 24'
(3) 56° 14'/82° 56'   (4) 54° 47'/83° 42'
(5) 51° 47'/83° 50'   (6) 50° 21'/83° 34'
(7) 49° 41'/83° 11'   (8) 50° 49'/82° 18'

No matter at which location you start, the aliens' main fort is always close to the Pole of Relative Inaccessibility at 53° 00'/83° 00', and their communications fort is located several miles to the east near 51° 20'/83° 00'. Although the *Arcticfox* manual states that destruction of the communications fort will "make it easier for you to approach the Main Fort," the damage you may suffer while trying to accomplish this could make you much more vulnerable when you tangle with the defenses around the main fortress. If you do plan an assault on the communications fort, starting location 5 or 6 will put you in good position for a quick strike.

First Strike

As soon as the game starts, launch a missile to destroy the heavy tank that you'll find directly in front of your Arcticfox. Then, leaving your heading directly south, increase your speed to 144kph and, while holding the joystick forward, press the P key to activate the Cannon Inclination Mode. In this mode, you'll continue to move forward at 144kph, and you can use your joystick to steer the Arcticfox and raise or lower the cannon. Remember that your cannon turret can't be rotated independently of the tank, so you must steer toward anything you want to hit. You should also note that once in the Cannon Inclination Mode, you can use Relative Reverse to change direction quickly or move forward at maximum speed from a dead stop.

If you watch the radar screen as you head southward across the snowfield, you'll see your Arcticfox pass between a horizontal ridge to the west and a green tundra field to the east. As you continue southward, the first enemy activity that you may see on the radar screen is a couple of blips approaching the Arcticfox from the east. Ignore them. Usually, these enemies—a light tank and recon sled—can easily be outrun. If they begin closing in on your tank, just drop off a couple of mines and that should take care of them.

Narrow Escape

Continue southward, keeping an eye on the position indicator. When you reach 53° 33'/82° 15', you should be able to spot an alien recon flyer maneuvering toward you from the southwest. Raise your gunsight as far as possible above the horizon and steer directly toward the plane. At first the enemy will appear almost as an indistinguishable black spot, but as soon as you can make out both wings jutting from the fuselage, use your 150mm cannon to blast him out of the sky. Once you fire, cut hard to the left to avoid the plane's tracking device.

When the danger has passed, turn back to the right so that you're heading directly to the southwest again. If you fail to down the recon flyer, he may attach a tracking device to your tank. If this happens, the radar indicator will turn red, and you'll hear a high-pitched ringing. While it's better to go undetected by the enemy for as long as possible, getting tagged with a tracking device doesn't significantly reduce the chances of a successful mission. What's more, there's really nothing you can do to get rid of the tracking device once it's attached, so your only option is simply to proceed with your battle plan as if nothing had happened.

Now continuing to the southwest, use the radar screen to guide you as you steer between two small ridges. As you pass between them, your position indicator should read 53° 13'/82° 25'. Up ahead, you'll be able to spot a rock and, to the south, another ridge about the size of the two you just passed between. As you near this ridge, you'll be able to spot a radar station and an air converter on the horizon. Just before you reach this ridge, dig your Arcticfox into the snow and fire a missile to destroy the radar station. Failure to eliminate this station will cause the alien defenses to become invisible to your radar. Often, you can take out both the radar station and the air converter with a single shot if you aim to hit the right side of the radar station. Once the radar station has been destroyed, dig out and continue directly southward.

Enemy Response

Before long, you'll approach a large tundra field with a crevice running from the field's northeast corner down to the southeast. Almost simultaneously, you'll pick up several blips moving toward you. This is the alien welcoming committee, and the fastest moving blips are fighters. Steer toward the fighters and try to shoot one or both down as they approach. More importantly, try to avoid their missiles by turning sharply as they pass overhead.

Once they've passed, turn toward the northeast corner of the tundra field. You'll notice that the crevice doesn't quite reach the tundra and that there is a small space where the snowfield continues unbroken to the south (52° 59'/82° 44'). This is the path you want to take. By staying on the snow, you'll be able to move faster than the alien tanks that are in the tundra.

As you look southward from the tip of the crevice, you'll notice a narrow strip of tundra up ahead with a second crevice along its southern edge. To the southwest, a large ridge rises above the frozen plain. Just as you reach the strip of tundra, launch a missile and guide it to the other side of the crevice where a tank and recon sled sit waiting. If they're close enough together, you may be able to take out both of them with one missile. Otherwise, just worry about the tank.

The Final Thrust

Once the tank has been destroyed, continue southward over the tundra. If any tanks follow you, be sure to drop off a couple of mines to keep them from getting too close. Steer slightly to the west toward the northeast corner of the ridge. As you approach the top of the ridge, be ready to blast any floating mines that might be guarding this area. While still on the ridge, activate the Dig In function. Although nothing will happen immediately, once you have reached the other side of the ridge, the Arcticfox will dig itself into the snow. This is important because, if you continue southward, the Arcticfox could be destroyed by floating mines launched from the main fort. The fort is also protected by a single rocket launcher capable of hitting your tank, even when it's buried in the snow. If you still have at least four missiles left, you should use one of them to take out the rocket launcher before attacking the main fort.

It's important to hit the fort's diamond-shaped top. It takes two direct hits to destroy the main fort, so as soon as the first missile hits, fire a second along the same flight path. Once the main fortress has been destroyed, the action continues for a few seconds, so there's still a chance that the Arcticfox could be destroyed. Either stay underground until it's over and pray you don't get bombed by a fighter, or come out firing and try to boost your score even further before the scenario ends. Either way, your final score should be at least 25,000.

25
Mech Brigade

In this platoon-level simulation of the future, NATO forces and the Soviets fight it out. You can play against another person, against the computer, or let the computer control both sides.

Every time I play *Mech Brigade*, I see the following picture: Like a scene straight out of one of those slick recruitment commercials, a small unit of M113 armored personnel carriers rolls over the hillsides of West Germany en route to the front. Inside one of the APCs, ten young grunts wearing green flak vests and helmets carry the usual accoutrements—automatic assault rifles, grenades, folding shovels, bayonets, mess kits, and so on. In addition, each soldier is busy planning for the attack using the most important weapon of all—the pocket calculator.

"Let's see, that would be (90 + (weapon accuracy × turns fired)) squared/100. Then I'll divide by 3 since they'll be in the woods, and then again by 2 + (speed/10) if they're moving. Does anyone have a spare roll of paper tape?"

Finally, an excited young soldier jumps up, banging his head on the low ceiling. "Sarge, I've got it. If I fire my M-16 from point-blank range at the rear of a T-72 for three minutes, I'll have a 45.38-percent chance of knocking out a tail light."

While war games, both computerized and the more traditional board variety, must depend on mathematics to govern range, sighting, and kill probabilities, sometimes it seems like SSI goes out of its way to make its games unfathomable to everyone without an advanced degree in integral calculus. In fact, such things as including a 26-line BASIC program to calculate direct fire/kill probabilities against armored vehicles only makes games like *Mech Brigade* and *Kampfgruppe* appear completely unplayable to the novice.

It's important to remember that your enjoyment of games like *Mech Brigade*, and the skill with which you play, depends more on your developing a general sense of which weapons are most effective against specific enemy forces at a particular range, and less on the exact kill probabilities in a given situation. This sense is developed not only by studying the maximum penetration, shell size, ranges, armor, and defense ratings of the various artillery, tanks, and antitank guided missile (ATGM) systems, but also by simply playing and experimenting on a tactical level.

Weapon Selection

When playing one of *Mech Brigade*'s four scenarios, you must do your best with the forces the computer assigns you. When building your own scenarios, however, you're given a number of selection points (SPs) to buy the companies, battalions, and regiments you think can best achieve your military objectives.

If you decide to play a small-meeting engagement using new U.S. forces, for example, you'll be given 50 SPs and shown a menu of eight packages—including a tank company, a mechanized company, cavalry troop, and, if the computer has decided to give you air superiority, a helicopter squadron. Unfortunately, the exact number and type of units you get in each package isn't listed in the game manual, so you have to select a package, exit to the deployment phase, then cycle through your forces to see what you got. A sample list of the packages and their contents for a small-meeting engagement using new U.S. forces appears in Table 25-1.

Although each package offers a good selection of weapons, during the deployment phase, you should always replace any weapons you know to be particularly ineffective against the Soviet forces you're likely to meet. For example, the Sergeant Yorks that invariably make up the third unit in each package are as much a disappointment in this game as they were to the Defense Department. You should replace them with something a little sportier, like Abrams battle tanks.

Table 25-1. New U.S. Formations Available for a Small-Meeting Engagement

(The number in parentheses is the Selection Point cost of each package.)			
Tank Co (14)	**Mech Co (16)**	**Cav Troop (26)**	**Cav Plt (8)**
3 M577	3 M577	3 M577	3 M577
4 Roland	4 Roland	4 Roland	4 Roland
4 Sg York	4 Sg York	4 Sg York	4 Sg York
2 Abrams	2 Bradley	3 Bradley	3 Bradley
4 Abrams	4 Bradley	5 Stinger	20 Rifle
4 Abrams	30 Bradley	3 M106	3 Dragon
4 Abrams	3 Dragon	3 Bradley	2 M901
	4 Bradley	20 Rifle	4 Abrams
	30 Rifle	3 Dragon	
	3 Dragon	2 M901	
	4 Bradley	4 Abrams	
	30 Rifle	3 Bradley	
	3 Dragon	20 Rifle	
		3 Dragon	
		2 M901	
		4 Abrams	
		3 Bradley	
		20 Rifle	
		3 Dragon	
		2 M901	
		4 Abrams	
DS Art Bn (10)	**GS Art Bn (9)**	**AH Sqn (24)**	**AD Battery (12)**
3 M577	3 M577	3 M577	3 M577
4 Roland	4 Roland	4 Roland	4 Roland
4 Sg York	4 Sg York	4 Sg York	4 SG York
3 M577	3 M577	4 Apache	3 M577
8 M109	8 M110	4 Apache	4 Sg York
8 M109	8 M110	4 Apache	4 Sg York
8 M109			4 Sg York
			4 Sg York

Deployment

When you deploy your forces before the start of a battle, begin in the center of the objective area and move the cursor around the 19 × 19-square area, paying close attention to the terrain. You'll want to give your advancing forces plenty of cover as they move toward the objective.

Since all self-propelled artillery units such as the M109s and 110s have virtually unlimited range, place these units well

behind the front lines. Divide your tanks, ATGMs, and infantry into at least two main contingents—one to approach the
objective from the north, and the other, from the south. This
way, when an enemy force is encountered, it will turn to face
one group while the other closes in from the rear to take advantage of the weaker rear and side armor.

Keep each combat formation's headquarters to the rear,
but within five squares of its units (ten if there's an open line
of sight between them). The Command HQ should be to the
rear of your main battle groups, preferably on a hilltop so that
it can easily request artillery fire.

Winning Without a Calculator

Although you don't really have to be a mathematician to be a
successful *Mech Brigade* general, you do have to understand a
couple of things about how the game works. The first is *command control*. If a combat formation's HQ is destroyed, or if a
unit is more than five squares from its HQ (ten with an unbroken line of sight), then the unit will not be in command control and the unit's movement and bombardment orders will be
delayed. When two boxers with equal power square off, it's
usually the one who's quicker on his feet and able to unload
his punches the fastest who'll win—it's much the same on the
battlefield.

Continuing the analogy, each punch a boxer takes slows
him down a little, dulls his concentration, and generally
makes his next punch slightly weaker. This is the way *suppression* works. As suppression increases, a unit's ability to move,
search for new targets, and hurt the enemy is diminished. Because suppression is cumulative within a single pulse, you
should keep the pressure on until suppression reaches the
maximum—200 for nonarmored units such as rifles, and 50
for vehicles. Once a unit's fully suppressed, however, you
should move a stronger unit into the square to deliver the
knockout punch.

Keep in mind that kill probabilities work similarly to suppression in that the more times a unit fires at the same enemy
unit, the greater the likelihood that you'll get a kill. Therefore,

you should always press T to check whether a unit has already selected a target, and whether the target has been fired on, before assigning a new one. Although an enemy unit may seem impervious to your attacks at first, repeated hits—particularly from more than one weapon type—can quickly wear down an enemy, and before long, the kills start occurring in greater and greater numbers. It's not unusual, for example, to get as many as five or six kills at one time on a rifle unit that's fully suppressed and hit repeatedly with heavy cannon fire from the same tank unit.

Don't let your units pick their own targets. During each orders phase, check all your active units to make sure their targets, ranges, facing, movement objectives, and speed all coincide with your overall strategy. Be especially careful whenever you have to move any units away from the enemy, because they'll turn in the direction they're moving and, in doing so, expose the weaker back armor to attack. If you have to move directly away from the enemy, be sure to readjust your units' facing as soon as they reach their destination.

★★ Scenario: Oldenburg, May 26, 1990 ★★

NATO Strategy

As the scenario begins, most of your forces are already in the objective area to the southeast of its center, at square (25,13). All units are facing east, and their ranges are set to 0. Although not yet visible, the Soviet forces are massed to the east and southeast, ready to launch a major assault on the objective area. You can expect four or five large T-72 units, several BMP-1s loaded with infantry, and a few BRDMs following in the rear as recon units.

In addition, far behind the lines to the northeast of these advancing forces are the Soviet self-propelled mortars—a unit of 6 BTRs that can bombard your infantry from 28 squares away. Other Soviet artillery includes 18 M-1973s divided into 3 units of 6. If these aren't flushed out, they can remain hidden and help to suppress your forces throughout the scenario.

Defense

Taking your combat formations A–I one at a time, here's how you should defend against the assault.

Because A0 is your Command HQ, you'll want to move it to a safer location to the west, but still within the objective area. Both A1 and A2 are Rapier-type surface-to-air missile units and can be fired only at the Soviet's Hind-D helicopters. Because there aren't any helicopters in this scenario, however, their only use is that they'll give you 10 points, each, if still in the objective area at the end of the game. Therefore, you may want to load A2 into a free MCV80, to transport it to the west and out of danger.

The next thing you want to do is to get your two FV432-Ms (B5 and B6) to begin bombarding suspected Soviet positions behind the line of forest squares that runs to the southeast. Use the local HQ (B0) as the requester because this will result in the shortest delay—only two pulses. As the battle progresses, other units will probably have an open line-of-sight to the bombardment target and, therefore, may be able to improve the accuracy of the bombardments. However, using any unit other than the combat formation's HQ will result in a longer delay. Hitting the enemy quickly is more important than boosting your accuracy. After all, it does you no good to be right on the money if the enemy has long since moved out of the target square. Also, forget using smoke. Though smoke can sometimes be useful to cover your tracks when you're on the move, in this situation, you want to do some damage—not simply fog up the enemy's glasses.

Next, set the ranges on your Milan ATGMs (B1–B4) on maximum. This way, as soon as the Soviet BMP-1s become visible, the Milans will begin launching on their own. Then, on subsequent turns, you can start selecting specific targets for them. Use your Spartans (B7) to sneak behind Soviet lines to spot enemy units to possibly divert their attention and fire away from your main forces on the edge of the city. Finally, your Blowpipes (B8) are in the same boat as your Rapiers and can be moved westward. Unlike the Rapiers, however, your Blowpipe unit can travel (slowly) on its own.

★★ *Mech Brigade* ★★

Your C formation is a loosely scattered group of MCV80s
and their disembarked infantry. Most of these units are in
good position to ambush the Soviet forces as they begin
breaking through the forest and charging over the hill where
C3 and C4 are set up. Therefore, leave the entire formation's
range set to 0 and just wait for the Russians to march through.
If you begin firing early, the Soviet artillery will try to soften
up these positions before the Soviet troops arrive.

Similarly, combat formations D, E, and F are all
MCV80/Rifle formations and you should use the *all-units*
mode to advance D and F into the city from the southwest
and northwest, respectively. Since all three formations are well
behind the front lines, you can set their ranges to maximum
without worrying about giving their positions away. From the
city, move these formations to the southeast to build a solid
line of defense against the advancing Soviet forces.

Your Chieftains (G0–G4) pose a more difficult problem.
They're powerful and have a slightly longer range than the
Soviet T-72s. It's tempting to set their ranges to the maximum,
hoping to knock out a few tanks before they're close enough
to strike back. Once the BMP-1s home in on the Chieftains
with their Sagger ATGMs, however, suppression quickly rises
and entire units of these British tanks are wiped out surprisingly fast. Perhaps the best solution is a compromise. Keep G0
and G4 in reserve, and set the others to the maximum range.
Because G4 is much farther east than the others, it's in a better
position to ambush the advancing forces anyway, and even
turn to blast the weak backsides of any Soviet units that slip
by. Since G0 is the formation's HQ, it should be committed to
combat only if the Soviets enter the city and are mixing it up
with your infantry.

ATGMs such as the Swingfires on your FV438s should be
set to their maximum ranges with the exception of the HQ
unit. The FV438s make up the H combat formation and are all
positioned in the south to thin out the T-72s and BMP-1s that
attack from the southeast.

The I formation consists of a Spartan HQ unit and five
Scimitar units that have been chosen for a top-secret mission.
It's up to this formation to sneak behind enemy lines and

eliminate the Soviet BTRs. To accomplish this, give them, as their first movement objective, a point on the northeast perimeter of the city, say, in the vicinity of square (33,5). The second movement objective will be about 3200 yards (16 squares) to the east. From here, you'll be able to spot the BTRs, and the Scimitars will be in range to open up fire. Just be sure to put on the brakes by setting the formation's movement speed to 0 once you reach the first objective.

Make sure most of the Soviet forces have already committed themselves to the westward push, and then continue on to the BTRs. Even if a couple of Soviet units do turn to fire a few shots as you pass to the north, most of your Scimitars will make it to the BTRs and easily wipe out the entire unit.

If it's still fairly early in the scenario once the BTRs have been taken care of, send the Scimitars south to deal with the Soviet M1973s in the same manner. Otherwise, you may simply want to bring the I formation back to the west, following the path in the forest through which some of the Soviet units just attacked. If timed right, this will stop the Soviets' forward movement toward the city, and it will allow your Scimitars, or the forces that stayed behind in the west, to hit the enemy's weaker rear armor. It's important to bring your reserve infantry formations (D, E, and F) to the front early, to bring as much force as possible to the defense of the objective area.

Soviet Strategy

The first order of business for the Soviet player is to strike hard and fast to prevent the NATO player from consolidating forces into a cohesive line of defense. Even though the NATO forces occupy the objective area at the start of the scenario, since your units are more unified, you have the opportunity to quickly bring a lot of combat strength to bear against small clusters of NATO defense. Consequently, a moment's hesitation or indecision on the part of the NATO player can give you the chance to begin breaking down the defenses one piece at a time.

First, use the heavy artillery of your K formation to bombard the area in and around the NATO entrenchments on the east edge of the city. This is where the NATO player's Milan ATGMs are located at the start of the game, and with any luck, you can keep these units suppressed and ineffective through much of the scenario. Next, using the *all-units* mode, order most of the other (nonartillery) formations near the southern map edge to move northwestward to just over the small hill between you and the objective area. Be aware, however, that there are a few isolated NATO units in place on the hilltop. Set the range on your T-72s (K1–K5) to maximum, and as soon as targets can be selected, go after the NATO MCV80s and FV438s. As your BMPs from combat formations G, H, and I begin to arrive within sighting range of the NATO forces, use their Sagger ATGMs to stop the Chieftans in their tracks.

Use your ZSU23/4s (A1) to support your front-line forces from 12 to 15 squares to the rear. Although primarily an anti-aircraft system, the ZSUs can be fired with some effectiveness at ground targets. And since there are no helicopters in this scenario, it's about all you can use them for anyway.

On the other hand, your SA-7s are similar to the NATO player's Rapiers in that they can only be fired at helicopters. Therefore, just before your BMP-1s break through the woods, you should unload your SA-7s for safekeeping. Halfway through the scenario, order them to begin moving into the objective area. Although some of these SAM units are bound to be eliminated, those that make it in and last until game's end will be worth ten victory points each.

If you can manage to eliminate most of the NATO Chieftans, Milans, and FV438s, charge right in and use your BMPs and RPG-7-equipped infantry to battle it out with the MCV80s and their infantry. You have a definite manpower advantage and, in a long battle, should be able to outlast your opponent.

26
Ogre

A monster machine from the future is loose and only you can stop its mad advance. Ogre *sets you in front of a computer-controlled battleship on land. Slow it down, disable its missiles and guns, and penetrate its armor, or you're likely to be ground under its nuclear-powered treads.*

★★ Preset Field 1 ★★
Mixed Defense vs. Mark III Ogre

Like *Arcticfox*, *Ogre* pits a lone supertank against an assortment of defenders. In both games, the tank's mission is to destroy the defenders' main fortress or, in this case, command post. The defenders' job is to eliminate the tank. This is where any similarity between the two games ends.

Arcticfox is basically a first-person shoot-em-up that makes you tank commander. *Ogre*, on the other hand, is a solitaire game that puts you in charge of the defensive forces. Instead of a vast Antarctic snowfield, *Ogre*'s battles are waged on a 21 × 15-hex map littered with craters and rubble.

Like most good games, *Ogre* is easy to learn to play, yet almost impossible to master. One reason is that although the Ogre's strategy varies little from game to game, the results of most attacks are decided by a roll of the computer's random-number generator. Because games are short (compared with most strategic war games), a few unlucky breaks can often mean the difference between victory and defeat.

The Combatants

The Ogre comes in both a Mark III and a Mark V model. The Mark III is equipped with two expendable long-range missiles, one main battery, four secondary batteries, and eight antipersonnel weapons. The more powerful Mark V carries six missiles, two main batteries, six secondary batteries, and 12 antipersonnel weapons.

In the beginning, both Ogres can move three hexes per turn. For each one-third of the cybertank's treads that are destroyed, its speed is reduced by one hex per turn. The Mark III starts the battle with 45 treads compared with 60 for the Mark V.

To defeat the Ogre, you must destroy all of its weapon systems as well as its treads. The probability of a successful attack against a specific weapon depends on the ratio of the attacking weapon's offensive strength to the defending weapon's defensive strength. This number is expressed as a percentage and is displayed at the bottom of the sidebar before you actually pull the trigger. The chances of any weapon hitting and destroying any of the Ogre's treads, however, is always 33 percent.

When defending against the Mark III, you're given 12 armor units and 20 infantry squads. If you take on the more formidable Mark V, though, you command 20 armor units and 30 infantry squads. In either case, your chances of destroying one of the Ogre's weapon systems is improved by combining firepower from various armored units. Only the infantry can launch combined attacks against the Ogre's treads, however, and only squads from the same group can be combined. Even when you attack the Ogre's treads using combined infantry units, the probability of a hit remains only 33 percent. If the attack is successful, one tread will be destroyed for each unit firing.

Defensive Equipment

One reason *Ogre* is such an easy game for new players to learn is that, besides infantry, there are only four types of defensive units—heavy tanks, missile tanks, ground effect vehicles (GEVs), and howitzers.

Heavy tanks are a little quicker than missile tanks, and slightly stronger both offensively and defensively. However, a missile tank can hit the Ogre from four hexes away, while the heavy tank must come within two hexes. GEVs, on the other hand, are the weakest armored unit, but have the advantage of two movement phases to just one for every other unit (including the Ogre). Under some circumstances, GEVs can sneak up to within firing range of the Ogre, blast away, and then scramble back to just beyond the Ogre's range. Howitzers, which count as two armor units, have the greatest range and firepower of any defensive weapon. But because these units are immobile and have virtually no defensive strength, you can generally kiss them goodbye once an Ogre gets close enough to return fire.

Battlefield Terrain

The *Ogre* battlefield is a 21 × 15-hex grid strewn with craters and rubble that, according to the game manual, are the result of "past nuclear detonations." Neither the Ogre nor any of the defending units can move over or through any hex containing a crater. Furthermore, rubble along the edges of hexes can't be crossed by any of the defensive armored units. But because of the Ogre's tremendous size and the infantry's use of powered battlesuits, neither is affected by rubble.

Although the terrain doesn't have a major effect on the outcome of the battle, it does bear some consideration as you maneuver your forces around the battlefield. For instance, if you know you'll have to move a few extra hexes to bring an armored unit away from the rubble and into position to fire at the advancing Ogre, move it early before the Ogre can come to within firing range. Also, don't let your front-line armored units get hemmed in by the rubble, or the Ogre may be able to outrun them as it charges up the battlefield toward your command post. If possible, try to anticipate the Ogre's moves and leave yourself a clear path so that you can keep it in range.

Craters can sometimes be used to put a little extra distance between your armored units and the Ogre. For example, an Ogre slowed to two hexes per turn, who has only anti-personnel weapons remaining, can still retaliate against a heavy tank by running it over. (The tank must come within two hexes before firing.) If there's a crater between your heavy tank and the Ogre, you can still fire across the crater, but you'll be protected from an overrun because the Ogre would have to move three hexes to reach your tank.

Three Classic Defensive Strategies

If you're a long-time *Ogre* fan, you're probably already familiar with three of the most popular *Ogre* defensive strategies.

Multiple howitzer defense. Because the howitzer is the only weapon with a longer reach than the Ogre, and because it packs a more powerful punch than any other defensive weapon, some players load the battlefield with howitzers, hoping to slow and ultimately destroy the Ogre before it can reach and eliminate the defensive units. But since the howitzers lack defensive strength and mobility, this is a dangerous tactic. If the Ogre survives the initial attack with most of its weapons and tread sections intact, it can move in and easily wipe out the howitzers.

GEV-centered defense. Although the GEVs don't have the range or attack strength of the other defensive units, their shear speed can sometimes be used to launch a series of quick strikes against the Ogre. Some players try to build a defensive formation around several GEVs in order to slow down and destroy the Ogre, gradually, with repeated hit-and-run attacks. However, since a GEV must be within two hexes of the Ogre in order to strike, and can move only three hexes after it has fired, the maximum distance the GEV can be from the Ogre after firing is five hexes. Thus, if the Ogre still has at least one missile left (attack range of 5), it can strike back at the GEV without even moving. And as long as the Ogre is still traveling at 2–3 hexes per turn, its main battery (attack range of 3) can retaliate against a fleeing GEV. However, once an Ogre's movement has been slowed or its missiles and main battery are gone, the GEVs can really make the quick-strike assaults they're designed for.

Mixed defense. The standard defense is the mixed defense, which uses a good balance of infantry and armored units deployed evenly around the map. This gives the defensive player more flexibility and allows weapons combinations to be used simultaneously against the Ogre. At the same time, a mixed defense is more difficult for the Ogre to figure out, since it gives the defensive player a greater range of options.

This may also be the easiest defense for many players to implement because it presents fewer of the logistics and timing problems posed by the other defenses.

Winning Strategy

No matter which defensive deployment you use, the most effective way to win the battle is with a three-phase attack that first slows, then weakens, and finally stops the cybertank before it can reach the command post. To do this, you must first attack the Ogre's tread section to slow it down by at least one hex per turn. In the middle phase, make an all-out concerted effort to eliminate as many of the Ogre's weapons systems as possible. In the last phase of the attack, try to bring the crippled Ogre to a stand-still before going in for the final kill.

The only problem with this strategy is that the Ogre is so powerful, it can often destroy most of your front-line forces before you're able to shoot away a third of its tread. Thus, even if you do manage to slow the tank, it may still have enough firepower left to finish off your few remaining units, and can then roll in uncontested against your command post. Once at your command post, the Ogre can use any remaining weapon to destroy it, or simply crush it beneath its treads.

I prefer an approach that strikes first at the Ogre's main weapon systems—its missiles, main, and secondary batteries—to render the cybertank powerless to defend itself. Then, when the Ogre has been sufficiently weakened, I move in to shoot the treads right out from under it. While there's a chance that the fast-moving Ogre may still be able to reach and overrun the command post even with its main weapons gone, if the treads become the focus of the attack early enough, the Ogre has little chance of reaching its destination.

Preset Field 1 provides you with a good selection of forces that can be used to try out this strategy right away. Refer to the *Ogre* map at the beginning of the game in Figure 26-1. (From this point on, the top of the map is referred to as north, the bottom as south, and so on.) Notice that the defensive forces include tanks on the front line, and tanks, infantry, and two howitzers standing guard before the command post. There's not a single GEV on the map, so any thoughts of a hit-and-run attack are gone from the start.

Tactics

At first glance the opening position looks like a no-win situation. Both of your front-line heavy tanks on the right side of the field are within reach of the Ogre's missiles. All it has to do is move up three spaces and fire. Some players would look at this situation and reason that, because the Ogre has a longer range than all of the defensive front-line forces, and since there's no way to move your tanks close enough to the Ogre to fire the first shots, the Ogre will always have a first-strike advantage. As a result, you may be tempted either to back away from the Ogre, trying to pull it to within range of your howitzers, or charge gallantly toward the cybertank, hoping to survive the initial barrage. Neither tactic is wise, or even necessary. There's a simple way to insure that you draw first blood, and it's the key to winning the game.

Instead of advancing or retreating, simply leave the two heavy tanks on the right side of the field where they are. Even though the Ogre could hit both of these tanks using missiles, it won't. It realizes that once fired, the missiles are gone for good, so it'll try to conserve them for as long as possible. (It'll need them as it nears the howitzers.) Therefore, you can safely leave both of these tanks in place during your first movement phase.

Because the Ogre enters the map on the right side of the field, however, you should move the left side of the line to the right. Do this by moving your missile tank one hex to the northeast (actually, two hexes, because it has to go around the rubble). Then, move the first heavy tank on the left three hexes to the right to directly below the missile tank. Finally, the leftmost heavy tank can come three hexes to the right.

After the Ogre thinks for a few seconds, it'll move northward two hexes and turn control back over to you. This time, just move the leftmost heavy tank one hex to the southeast to further tighten the line. At this point the Ogre will respond by moving up three hexes and firing its main battery at your

Figure 26-1. *Ogre* map at beginning of play.

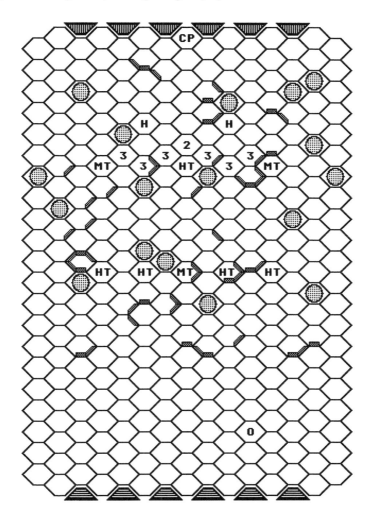

```
     O-Ogre
    CP-Command
     H-Howitzer
   MT-Missile Tank
   HT-Heavy Tank
  2,3-Infantry Squads
```

221

rightmost tank. That's it. If the Ogre misses, you'll be in a perfect position to move all of your front-line forces to within firing range at once, and use their combined firepower to begin weakening the Ogre.

If the Ogre's shot hits, however, you may want to restart the game because damaging the Ogre before it can disable any of your front-line forces is crucial to winning.

Prepare to Fire

Once you've moved your forces into position, fire all five weapons, one-by-one, at the Ogre's four secondary batteries. The reason you shouldn't go after the powerful, long-range missiles is that, as already mentioned, once they're fired, they're gone. And since there's only one main battery, wait until all four secondary batteries are gone before attacking it. Your heavy tanks must come within two hexes to hit the Ogre—the secondary batteries' shorter range doesn't make them any less dangerous.

With any luck, your four heavy tanks and one missile tank should be able to eliminate at least two of the secondary batteries. The Ogre will then move up one hex, try to wipe out one or two heavy tanks with its secondaries, and fire its main battery at your missile tank. Since you still haven't taken a shot at his missiles, the Ogre won't feel that they're in any danger, so it'll keep them holstered.

Continue to stay within range of the Ogre, but avoid bringing any of your forces closer than necessary to fire on the cybertank. Target its main and secondary batteries with your remaining units. Once these weapons have been destroyed, you may want to consider combining firepower against the Ogre's missiles. This is a good time for you to shift your second line tanks to the right and south. Ideally, you want to have the Ogre down to its last missile when it comes within range of your howitzers, so that it's forced to decide which one it'll take out.

The Ogre's eight antipersonnel weapons aren't priority targets. This doesn't mean that infantry units aren't important to winning the game. In fact, without them you'd probably never be able to stop the Ogre in time. It's just that since the antipersonnel weapons can be used only against infantry units and the command post itself, and because they have a range of only one hex, your firepower is put to much better use against the Ogre's treads and longer-range weapons.

By the time the Ogre reaches your infantry units, its major weapons should be gone, or at the least, nearly gone. Close in with as many three-unit infantry groups as possible, and combine all three units in each group on the Ogre's treads. In addition, any remaining howitzers, missile tanks, and heavy tanks should begin picking off those treads as well in an all-out effort to stop the Ogre in its tracks. Executed properly, these tactics will insure a win. With a little practice and some luck, you may even have enough units remaining at the end of the game to score a Complete Defense Victory.

★ PART 3 ★

GEOPOLITICAL DECISION MAKING

27
Balance of Power

Machiavelli would feel right at home in this simulation of modern super-power diplomacy. Insurgencies, coups, and intimidation must be balanced with the right mixture of pressure and support to friendly countries in order for you to win.

In a surprise move, the U.S.S.R. sends $100 million to aid insurgents in Peru. Outraged by the Soviet's attempts to topple the pro-American government, you immediately send a short note to the premier of the Soviet Union questioning the wisdom of his meddling in the affairs of a country that is clearly within the United States' sphere of influence. Insulted by your note, the Soviet premier reaffirms his country's position. You decide that Soviet interference of any kind in Peru cannot be tolerated, so you publicly challenge the Soviets on the issue. Unfortunately, the Soviets stand firm and you must now decide whether to escalate the affair from a diplomatic to a military crisis.

You decide to press your case, and before you realize what has happened, the United States and the Soviet Union are standing toe-to-toe on the brink of nuclear war. You are at DefCon 3, and the armed forces of both superpowers are on alert, prepared to go to combat on short notice. Back down now in front of a very attentive world, and you'll lose the respect of several smaller countries that had looked up to you as a symbol of strength and integrity. Dare the Soviets to back down once more, and World War III could begin and end in one big cloud of smoke.

On the Brink

That's the kind of situation that can quickly develop when you play Chris Crawford's *Balance of Power*. As president of the United States or premier of the Soviet Union, your objective is to increase your country's influence and international prestige while avoiding a nuclear war that will result in both sides losing. If you can survive your eight-year stint as president (presumably you are reelected after your first term) and end up gaining more prestige than your opponent, you win.

In addition to the two superpowers, 60 computer-controlled minor countries also occupy the world of *Balance of Power*. However, their roles in the simulation are basically those of pawns. If a minor power's government has warm relations with your country, you may try to protect it with treaties and through economic and military aid. If the government of a minor power isn't particularly friendly, you can either try to win it over with economic aid, apply diplomatic pressure, send in the CIA to stir up discontent among the locals, help fund insurgents operating in the country, or even send in troops to help overthrow the existing government.

Depending on the seriousness of the actions you take and the importance of the minor country to your opponent, you may be asked to reconsider your policy in the matter. Similarly, if you feel that your opponent's policy in a minor country is seriously out of line, you can demand that he or she back down. Initially, a challenge of this type by either superpower is a quiet affair, and backing down from your original position will cause you to lose no prestige. If neither side is willing to give in, however, the disagreement escalates to crisis proportions and attracts the attention of the rest of the world. In many cases, the prestige at stake can grow way out of proportion to the importance of the original issue, thus, putting you in a no-win situation.

Give and Take

But how do you know when you should stand your ground and when you should give a little for the sake of the planet? Before you make a policy decision that is likely to be challenged by the other superpower—or before you challenge your opponent—try to determine which of you has a greater commitment to the issue. If, after studying all of the available data, you feel that the minor power involved is important to your long-term success and of less value to your opponent, then go ahead and stand firm, especially if the country in question is solidly within your sphere of influence. If the opposite is true, then, unfortunately, you'll have to let the enemy have his or her way.

With many minor powers, however, there is no clear indication of which superpower will have the greatest commitment. In these cases, it is sometimes useful to carefully study the way the computer phrases replies. Look for subtle hints of uncertainty or signs that the opponent might reconsider his or her position if given a good enough reason. If you detect any such weakness, the computer can probably be forced to back down by challenging.

Finally, you can always consult your advisers to see who they feel has the greatest interest in the matter at hand. If you've done all of your homework by studying the world situation carefully, however, there's no reason to assume that your advisers' assessment of the situation has any more validity than your own. This is especially true when you're playing at the expert or nightmare levels.

Making Policy

To fulfill the first requirement of being a winner—achieving a greater level of prestige than your opponent—you must implement your policy decisions carefully and with thoughtful consideration of all likely consequences. Fortunately, *Balance of Power* usually provides you with more than enough information on each minor power and its relations with both superpowers to allow you to make policy intelligently, and to avoid the accidental dropping of political bombshells. The real secret to winning is in understanding and using this wealth of available data to guide your policy-making throughout the world.

For instance, before you initiate a policy that will affect a minor power, always check the country's Closeup display. Among other things, the Closeup display shows you the state of diplomatic relations between the minor country and each of the superpowers, any treaties that may be in effect, and whether the country is in the U.S. sphere of influence, the Soviet sphere of influence, or is neutral.

The most important thing to remember about spheres of influence is that it's best not to interfere in countries that are solidly within your opponent's sphere, and conversely, not to stand for your opponent's meddling in countries that are solidly within your own sphere. Obviously, the United States suddenly paying a lot of attention to Eastern-bloc, countries or the Soviets taking an interest in Latin America, would be viewed with suspicion and would probably result in a strong challenge by the opposition.

Another important factor to consider before involving yourself in the affairs of another country is the amount of prestige to be gained by getting that country on your side. Whether a minor power's relationship with your own country is friendly or hostile, it may simply not have a sufficient prestige value to be worth fighting over. The time to determine a country's worth as an ally is before you begin directing policy toward it.

Winning Friends and Eliminating Enemies

Assuming that a country isn't solidly within your opponent's sphere of influence and is worth enough prestige points to warrant your getting involved, the next step is to check the state of insurgencies within the country, the likelihood of a coup, and the chances that the country can be pressured into either your camp or your opponent's. This will help you to determine the best strategy for either keeping a friendly country in your corner or replacing a hostile government with one that is more to your liking.

Insurgencies

If the reports show a strong insurgency developing within an unfriendly country, you may want to provide economic aid to the insurgents. Funding an insurgency that ultimately fails, however, can be costly—both in dollars and prestige. Therefore, don't support any rebels unless you're fairly certain they can win and you can stand up to any challenges by your opponent.

Some insurgencies do very well on their own and can take out a hostile government without any outside assistance. For this reason, you should study an insurgency for a couple of turns before committing yourself to see how it progresses on its own. If it seems to have built its own momentum, or has reached civil war proportions, wait until the government is about to fall, and then kick in a few bucks to help finish it off.

When insurgencies occur in friendly countries and you'd like to do what you can to help the legitimate government crush the rebellion, consider whether or not your aid can have any real effect on the outcome. Many of the larger countries are perfectly capable of handling their own insurgents and honestly don't need your help. You're better off helping a smaller government that might benefit more from your assistance.

Honoring Commitments

While insurgents can be aided right up until their cause is won, you should take action early when you support a government, especially if you have a previous treaty with the country in trouble. Failure to meet any of your treaty commitments will result in a serious loss in prestige.

In some cases, it may be necessary to commit some of your own troops in support of an insurgency, or to help a weaker government remain in power. Intervening on behalf of insurgents or the current government of a country is a serious action and should never be attempted if the other superpower has already intervened. Also, never use military intervention as your first course of action. Always begin your involvement in foreign insurgencies by sending small amounts of aid. If increasing the amount of aid during subsequent years results in no major protests from your opponent, then you may be able to get away with sending in some troops.

One thing to keep in mind is that it's impossible to help out either side in an insurgency if you don't have troops stationed in a country that borders on the one where the insurgency is taking place. This logistical restriction makes it nearly

231

impossible to win *Balance of Power* if you play as an isolationist. To be successful, you must cultivate friendly relations with strategically placed nations around the world, and use these footholds to spread your influence to the countries where it's needed most.

Coups

As in the real world, governments are sometimes replaced without lengthy civil wars. Sometimes the leader is quietly removed from office by internal forces or driven out by disloyal factions of the military. In more democratic countries, a dissatisfied population can replace its leaders through legitimate elections. In *Balance of Power*, events such as these are considered coups and are caused primarily by an unacceptable standard of living within a country.

Although you can send in the CIA to "destabilize" an unfriendly country whose government you'd like to see replaced, there are other, more subtle ways of ripening a country for a coup. Diplomatic pressure can be useful in many cases. Another tactic is to make the government so nervous—by stationing troops in a neighboring country—that it will increase its military spending out of fear. Since every country has a limited amount of resources, any military build-up cuts into consumer spending and, thus, lowers the standard of living. Anything you can do to induce a government to increase its military spending will cut into its consumer spending and, therefore, cause unrest.

Conversely, you can often save friendly countries who are facing the threat of a coup by providing them with economic aid. Just remember that your money will go a lot further in a poor country than it will in a wealthy country. Once the danger of a friendly government being overthrown by a coup has passed, you can take the aid away to use somewhere else without really damaging relations.

Winning Through Intimidation

Unfortunately, many hostile countries have governments that are so firmly entrenched, they can't be subverted from within, through either insurgencies or coups. If the country is weak militarily, however, it is sometimes possible for you to intimidate the country into liking you (or at least pretending it does) through a combination of diplomatic and military pressure. This process is called *Finlandization,* and it depends, in part, on your projecting the image of a world-class bully. You can accomplish this by stationing large numbers of your troops around the world and becoming involved in many crises. Carefully monitor the target country's Closeup display to determine when it is close to Finlandizing. Then, don't be afraid to apply a little diplomatic pressure to help the process along.

Once you learn that a country has Finlandized to you, check to see whether it has canceled any treaties with your opponent. If so, you may want to jump right in and offer a security treaty to keep the country from flopping back in the opposite direction in response to pressure from your opponent. Just be prepared to stand by your treaties by providing the country with enough military and economic aid to make it feel secure.

Balancing Act

The name *Balance of Power* itself is a clue to the best general strategy for winning the game. You must always maintain a balance between reckless aggressiveness and passive isolationism. Go after those countries you feel you need to win, but don't think you can conquer the world in a day. Don't immediately challenge any policy your opponent makes without first examining all of the available data. Try to anticipate your opponent's next move as you would in a game of chess. Often, small policy decisions make sense only when viewed as part of a larger plan.

Implement your policies throughout the world a step at a time, first by moving into areas that offer the least resistance, and then by building on your early successes to create diplomatic momentum. Stand tough when you have to, but don't be afraid to back down, when necessary, to maintain the balance.

28
Geopolitique 1990

A game of diplomatic intrigue and strategy for world dominance,
Geopolitique is actually two games in one—the first phase involves
maneuverings between the superpowers and, if these fail, the second stage
is all-out war.

When I first decided to devote a section of this book to geopolitical war games, *Geopolitique 1990* was one of the first ti-
tles that came to mind. Although not nearly as complex as
Balance of Power, Geopolitique 1990 does a good job of simulat-
ing the U.S./Soviet struggle for economic, political, and military superiority, in a game format that takes into account the
resources, military strength, industrial capacity, and political
orientation of 16 "minor" countries.

Two Games
Geopolitique 1990 is actually two games in one. The first,
Geopol, is a diplomatic contest in which both major countries
evaluate their positions, decide how best to use their industrial
capacity, and employ military and political pressure to attain
economic, political, and military agreements with minor countries. This process is repeated during each yearly turn. The
winner is the country that first reaches a preset number of
GNP (Gross National Product), Prestige, and National Security
points. The relative importance of these three indicators is determined, in part, by how the player prioritizes them at the
start-up menu.

    The second game, Geowar, results when you or your
computerized Soviet opponent decide to declare war during
Geopol. To win Geowar, you must have at least 60 victory
points for two consecutive turns. The computer may win,

however, with any successful attack against the continental United States. A declaration of Geowar should usually be considered only as a last resort, however, since there is a built-in bias factor against the country that initiates the war.

Geopol

As the name implies, each of *Geopolitique 1990's* seven scenarios begins in 1990. Turns consist of six phases that, combined, represent a year of simulated time. The first order of business in each new year is to assess your current world position by checking how close you are to your economic, political, and military objectives. This information is represented by a horizontal bar chart with bars labeled GNP, Prestige, and Natl Secty, and with asterisks marking your objectives. Similar information on the Soviet goals is also displayed, but without the asterisks. Thus, you're never quite certain exactly where their priorities lie. Figure 28-1 shows U.S. and Soviet Union positions.

Figure 28-1. U.S. and U.S.S.R. Status

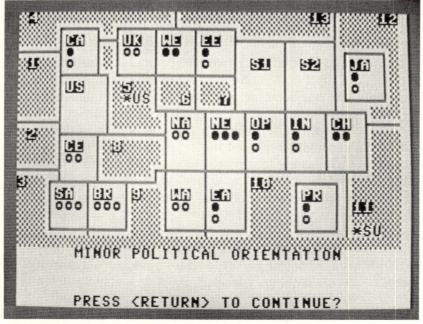

Planning Is Key

Next, you review three reports that show your military presence throughout the world, the political orientation of the game's 16 minor countries, and any agreements both major powers have with these countries. Understanding and using the data contained within these three reports is crucial to your success. Although the report on your military presence is of limited value at this stage, knowing the political orientation of the world's minor countries will prevent you from wasting your time seeking diplomatic agreements with countries that are very pro-Soviet. At the same time, being able to identify countries that are pro-Western, or even neutral, gives you some diplomatic targets to aim for.

Similarly, knowing the economic, political, military, and neutrality agreements that both major powers have already made with the minor countries lets you determine, in advance, the topics that will be open for discussion in the next negotiation phase. Therefore, the overall purpose of studying these reports is to decide with which minor countries you will try to reach agreements, and what types of agreements you intend to discuss.

Industrial Production

After viewing your reports, you can either declare war on the U.S.S.R. or move to the next phase of Geopol, where you'll decide what portion of your total industrial capacity (both foreign and domestic) you will allocate to raw material production, and how much you'll reserve for the production of secondary goods. The amount you choose to devote to raw material production must then be further distributed among three raw materials—food, metal, and energy.

Industrial capacity devoted to secondary goods production is similarly divided among four categories. The first is military maintenance and is determined by the number of military task forces you have operating around the globe. If you're not able to maintain your current military presence, you have to demobilize some of your forces. This is also an option if you simply want to free up some of your industrial capacity points to fund other activities. On the other hand, you may choose to mobilize additional military units, especially if you are having a hard time reaching your military goals.

Political Action Points

The third way to use your industrial capacity is to produce political action points (PAPs). During the Geopol Decision Phase, you can use the PAPs purchased here to buy your way into a bargaining position with some of the minor countries. To remain competitive with the Soviet Union, you should always try to buy at least four PAPs. Finally, you may put some of your industrial capacity back into industry so that even greater industrial capacity can be enjoyed in subsequent years.

The interesting thing about this phase of Geopol is the way raw material production relates to secondary goods production. The total amount of industrial capacity you devote to food, metal, and energy, as well as the distribution you establish among these commodities, has a direct relation to the amounts of industrial capacity you can spend on each of the secondary goods. Generally, you should begin with an even split between natural resources and secondary goods, and then study where the shortages and surpluses occur. With each subsequent turn, try to adjust the amounts allocated to food, metal, and energy so that you can purchase your secondary goods without any shortages or surpluses of these three raw materials.

Military Deployment

In the next phase of Geopol, you get to place your military task forces in any of the game's 13 ocean areas. Now, keeping in mind the minor countries, which, from the reports you read earlier, looked like good negotiation targets, you should position your task forces in adjacent ocean areas where their presence will have, let us say, a "favorable" effect on negotiations. Often, if things break down at the bargaining table, you're given the option of declaring a limited war against the minor country, provided, of course, that you have a task force on standby in an adjacent ocean, and you have no previous military agreements with the country.

Once your forces are in place, it's time to apply the PAPs you bought earlier. One or two PAPs may be placed in any minor country with which you want to negotiate in the upcoming negotiation phase. Likewise, the Soviets will get to put their two cents in at this time, and the major power with the majority of PAPs in a minor country wins the right to negotiate agreements there. Be aware that the U.S.S.R. likes to put a lot of their industrial capacity into PAPs and spread them around, so that in each negotiation phase, they get to sit down at the bargaining table with a lot of minor countries. Pay attention to where they place their task forces during the military placement phase for an indication of the countries with which they will seek negotiations. You can then use your available PAPs to try to outbid them, or else you can go after only those minor countries in which the Soviets have no interest.

Negotiations

When you finally get to the negotiations phase and sit down with a minor country to hammer out an economic, political, or military agreement, you'll have a choice of five negotiating strategies, ranging from a simple request to the threat of military action. To help you decide the approach to take, the negotiation screen provides information on the minor country's military strength, political orientation and stability of its government, any previous agreements that the country may have with you or the Soviet Union, and the number of prestige points that are at stake for both major powers. Generally, the harder you push for an agreement, the more prestige there is at stake. Figure 28-2 shows the negotiation screen.

With pro-Western countries, a simple request is usually the best way to start negotiations. If the minor country responds by saying an agreement appears imminent, you can go ahead and upgrade your position to a strong request. This often results in an immediate closing of the deal. Neutral or pro-Soviet countries should be leaned on a little harder, however, but be sure you have the military strength to back up

Figure 28-2. Negotiation Screen

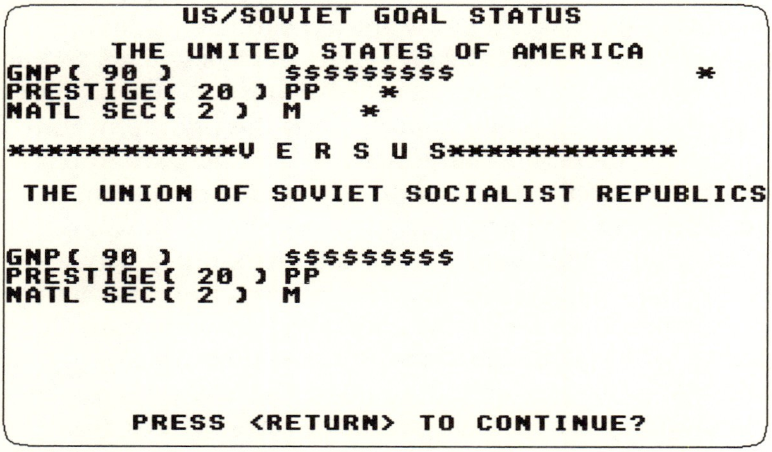

```
              US/SOVIET GOAL STATUS
         THE UNITED STATES OF AMERICA
GNP( 90 )       $$$$$$$$$                    *
PRESTIGE( 20 ) PP         *
NATL SEC( 2 )   M    *

*************V E R S U S**************

 THE UNION OF SOVIET SOCIALIST REPUBLICS


GNP( 90 )        $$$$$$$$$
PRESTIGE( 20 ) PP
NATL SEC( 2 )   M



        PRESS <RETURN> TO CONTINUE?
```

your tough talk—as you escalate your demands, there's no going back to a softer position. If the country has previous military agreements with the Soviets, don't be surprised if the U.S.S.R. intervenes in negotiations, or even comes to the country's defense in the event of a limited war.

Geowar

Various events that occur during Geopol—such as limited wars, the replacement of moderate Soviet Politburo members with more militaristic members, and the deployment of new task forces—can result in an increase in the world tension level. When world tension reaches Level IV, the diplomatic atmosphere is considered very tense, and if you don't declare war on the Soviet Union, there's a real good chance they'll declare war on you.

If Geowar is initiated by either major power, the world's minor countries will either declare their neutrality or announce their support for one of the major powers. Then, as in Geopol, Geowar requires you to start by deciding how to use your industrial capacity. This time, however, there are only three choices. You can reinforce your land, naval, and air strength;

you can produce military units to add to those already deployed; or you can sink some of your industrial capacity back into industry in order to boost your industrial capacity for the next turn.

After selecting the units that will receive reinforcements, you get to move your military units from their present locations to adjacent areas. During this phase, armies can be "transferred" to areas that aren't adjacent as long as friendly fleets occupy ocean areas in an unbroken chain from the army's original area to its destination. Finally, newly mobilized units must be designated as either armies or fleets.

Collecting Strategic Data

To help you make strategic decisions concerning the movement and deployment of your forces, four reports are available. The first shows the location of all U.S. and Soviet armies and fleets. Another report shows the total victory points for both major powers and the degree of control each has in every area of the world. The third is a status report that lists all of your forces along with their strengths, and the last report shows which major power has air superiority in each area.

This last report will help you in your final task, before entering the attack phase, which is to decide how to allocate your available air strength. In a process similar to the allocation of PAPs during Geopol, you select minor countries or ocean areas as the targets for all of your units capable of carrying out air operations. The computer then calculates which major power has air superiority in each area, and to what degree.

The importance of air superiority is three-fold. First, without air superiority in an area, you'll be unable to launch amphibious assaults against that area. Second, by maintaining air superiority in an area, you can expect to intercept about 50 percent of the enemy reinforcements headed for that area. Third, air superiority is figured into a unit's overall strength and, consequently, can have a great effect on the outcome of a battle.

Another factor that influences the outcome of any battle is the terrain occupied by the defender. In open areas such as

Canada and Central America, the defending units' defense strength is actually only 80 percent of what it would normally be. On the other hand, defending an area that has rought terrain, like East or West Africa, multiplies the defensive strength of your forces by 1.2, thus increasing it by 20 percent. Similarly, urban areas like China, the United States, and the United Kingdom increase the defensive strength of your forces by 40 percent. Defensive strength is not affected by deserts such as those in northern Africa or the Near East, or the steppe region of the U.S.S.R.

Victory Is Ours

One of the keys to winning Geowar is achieving a few early victories. When you defeat a minor country, you gain both its victory points and, just as important, its economic resources. This will insure continued funding of the war effort during subsequent turns. What's more, a successful battle forces any defending Soviet units back into adjacent areas, and if all adjacent areas are also under attack, the losers must retreat all the way back to Mother Russia.

As with Geopol, once a major power achieves a significant lead during Geowar, it's difficult (if not impossible) to turn things around. Therefore, if you sense a slight edge, maintain the initiative. Most important, don't think that a weak or losing position during Geopol can be saved by declaring Geowar. The best time to go to war with the Soviets is when you have significant leads in all three of the major indicators—GNP, prestige, and national security.

29
Colonial Conquest

The nineteenth century brought as much jockeying for territory, among the major world powers, as did the fifteenth century's discovery of the New World. Diplomacy may have been the byword in the courts of Europe, but aggression was the rule of the day.

★★ 1880 Scenario ★★

During the late 1800s, the United States was beginning to emerge as a major world power, despite the fact that at just 100 years old, it was a relatively new kid on the block. Along with France, England, Germany, Russia, and Japan, the United States was vying for its share of the world's territories, through colonial expansion. It was a time of overt imperialism, when the major players shuffled troops around in a high-stakes poker game and used the world's minor countries as chips. Instead of secret plots and covert funding abroad, the United States, along with its European and Asian counterparts, relied primarily on direct military agression to extend its control.

Colonial Conquest simulates this Age of Imperialism on a color-coded scrolling map that divides the world into eight geographic areas. The six major countries mentioned above can be controlled by human players, assigned to computer-control, or relegated to the status of minor countries by designating them as neutral at the startup menu. To win, it isn't necessary for one player to gain control of all the other major countries. You need only to score a preset number of points by winning land and sea battles, and by gaining control of some of the world's minor countries.

The Big Buildup

Colonial Conquest is played in three main phases: a build phase, a movement phase, and a combat phase. Each player gets four turns a year, corresponding to the four seasons. Both the movement and combat phases take place during every turn. However, the build phase happens only once each year during the spring turn. During the build phase, you can use the money you've gained from the countries you control to do the following five things:

• Build up your army and navy.
• Fortify the position of any friendly troops you have stationed around the map.
• Provide neutral countries with economic assistance.
• Spy on your enemies.
• Fund a coup in a minor country that you wish to destabilize.

During the late nineteenth century, a major power didn't remain a major power very long without a strong military. Only by creating new army units at your supply centers can you hope to defend the territories already under your control, and extend your influence to new areas. Similarly, you can increase your status as a naval power by building fleets in any friendly port containing a supply center. The cost of building army units and fleets depends on the major country you control, and is consistant among the game's three scenarios. Often, the better an army's offensive and defensive ratings, the more it costs to buy troops.

For example, a player controlling England must pay $600,000 for 10,000 troops, compared with only $200,000 for 10,000 Russian troops. The Russian player really gets no bargain, however, since Russian troops have offensive and defensive ratings of 4 (the worst) and 3 respectively, while the English troops have a rating of 1 (the best) for both offense and defense. Unfortunately for the player controlling Russia, you don't always get what you pay for when it comes to buying fleets for your navy. Not only does the Russian navy have the worst offensive and defensive ratings of any major country, but it also costs the most to build—$700,000 per five fleets compared to only $300,000 for five English fleets, which, along with U.S. fleets, are tied for the best ratings.

Fortifications

Once you have some of your expensive troops positioned in key areas, you'll want to save some of your money ($1,000,000 to be exact) to fortify them. Fortification doesn't come cheap, but you'll have achieved two things for your money. First, you'll double the defensive strength of the territory you fortify, and second, you'll make it more costly for your enemies to spy on the fortified territory. Remember, if you put all your effort into expansion and don't protect what you already control, the other major countries can quietly sneak in the back door while you're looking toward the next big victory.

Economic Aid

Providing other major or minor countries with economic assistance can be risky business. If you loan money to another major country to put an end to a long and bloody war that you would eventually end up losing, the money is probably well spent. However, don't think a little economic aid is going to buy you a lifelong ally. If both you and the other country continue to struggle for dominance in the same area of the world, renewed warfare is inevitable.

Covert Activities

Whenever possible, it's best to avoid getting into dangerous situations that result in your having to dish out huge payoffs. One way to steer clear of such confrontations is to do some spying before you commit troops to an adjacent territory. In other words, look before you leap. During the espionage part of the build phase, a mere $200,000 will allow you to find out the approximate military strength of a minor country with an unfortified army. However, it costs five times that amount to check up on the supply centers of major countries or fortified armies. Since these are the last areas you would want to attack anyway, you should focus most of your espionage on minor neutral countries.

One way to gain control of some of the poorer minor countries is by undermining their military strength through subversion. When you spend money to subvert a minor country, you drain its military strength. Weaken the country's military enough and a coup will take place that can pave the way for your takeover. Whether or not there is a successful coup, the country's military strength will suffer. Although subverting a minor country doesn't directly add any victory points to your score, the additional income you receive from controlling the subverted country will help fund your future expansion in ways that can add to your score.

On the Move

After the spring build phase, and during each of the next three seasonal turns, you'll have an opportunity to move troops from the areas you control into other friendly territories, as reinforcements, or into adjacent areas that aren't under your control, but that you wish to attack. The actual fighting won't take place until the following combat phase, however, and troops that have been given movement orders become unavailable until they've reached their destination. Figure 29-1 is a map of the 1880 scenario.

Troops traveling over land are always limited to movement into adjacent territories, but troops carried by your fleets can move from one port to any other. Like troop movement between adjacent territories, troop movement between two ports can be used either to bring reinforcements into friendly areas, or to attack neutral or enemy ports. Fleets can also be sent without troops to harass enemy fleets. Such excursions are called naval *sorties*. When a sortie is over, the fleets involved return to their home port. Because no victory points are awarded for wins or losses by fleets without troops, you'll find the naval sortie of limited strategic use.

There are a few things to keep in mind as you enter each new movement phase. First, use any information you may have gathered during the espionage portion of the build phase to your advantage. That is, move some troops and fleets in to attack weak neutral territories, and try to reinforce those

Figure 29-1. The 1880 Scenario

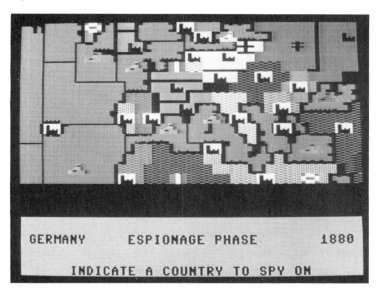

GERMANY   ESPIONAGE PHASE   1880

INDICATE A COUNTRY TO SPY ON

friendly territories that seem like probable targets for enemy attacks. Don't forget that because enemy troops can be transported by ship, your port territories are never really safe from attack.

Consider, too, the value rating of any country you are thinking of attacking. A country with an *A* rating will help to further your goals by adding to your net income faster than a country with a *D* rating. Value ratings are assigned randomly during the standard game, but the value ratings for all countries in effect for the two historical scenarios are listed in the *Colonial Conquest* player's manual, along with their overall defensive ratings.

Next, don't spread your existing forces too thin. Moving into as many neutral areas as possible early in the game is a great way to boost your income. However, it can take you several turns to move the troops you buy during the build phase from your supply centers to the outlying areas of your empire. If the area you control is growing so fast that you have a hard time supplying troops to defend it, you may want to put on the brakes for a while and concentrate on protecting what you have.

Finally, keep in mind that your first major goal should be to gain control of an entire region, since this will result in your receiving a large economic bonus. While this may seem to contradict the last piece of advice, it really doesn't. You should build toward this goal slowly and defend every inch of your empire (particularly your supply centers) as if an enemy attack is always imminent—it is. An empire that grows very rapidly without the support of strong defensive forces is bound to collapse under its own weight before the entire region can be secured.

Settling the Score

Once each of the six major countries has had a chance to issue movement orders to its troops and fleets, the combat phase begins. At this point, there's nothing you can do but sit and wait, hoping that the flashing flag in the territory you've decided to attack turns out to be yours. The computer keeps track of all the action and, when the fighting has stopped, determines the winner of all battles.

While it's obvious that numeric superiority plays a large part in the outcome of both land and naval battles, other factors are taken into consideration during victory determination. First, as mentioned earlier, the armies and navies of each major country have both offensive and defensive ratings that influence their performance in combat. These ratings, as well as the number of fleets and troops each country begins with, are listed in the table on the back page of the player's manual.

Terrain

Another factor that can affect the outcome of a battle is the terrain of the defending country. Terrain modifiers range from 0 (difficult to defend) to 4 (easy to defend) and are indicated on the scenario maps that come with the program. Notice that only a handful of minor countries, such as Brazil, Greece, and Arabia, are given ratings of 4, while several territories, particularly small islands like Midway, Canary Island, and Ceram, have ratings of 0. As might be expected, the majority of territories have terrain ratings in the 2–3 range. Keep these factors in mind when planning your expansion.

U.S. Strategy

In the 1880 scenario, the player who controls the United States has one advantage over the other major countries: three supply centers compared with only two (except Russia, which has only one). In addition, with offensive and defensive factors of 2 for the army and 1 for the navy, the U.S. military ability seems as good, or better, than that of every other major country except England. Unfortunately, although the quality of the U.S. military in the 1880 scenario is excellent, the quantity is lacking. A comparison of the actual numbers of troops and fleets shows that in 1880, the United States was behind in the arms race. England not only had the best forces, it also had the most.

The English Threat

To make a difficult situation even worse, England starts the scenario right on your doorstep in the best position to sweep down over the United States like a plague. With control of the Canadian provinces of Alberta, Quebec, Manitoba, and Ontario, as well as the Hudson Bay and the Western Territory, England is in a perfect position to launch a campaign against your four U.S. territories. It could be it a very short game.

Two things work in your favor, however. The first is the fact that for the first three to seven years of a scenario, the computer-controlled countries are more interested in taking over all the minor countries than in attacking major countries. The second is the generally poor defensive ratings in effect throughout most of Canada. The combination of these two factors allows you virtually to eliminate the English presence in North America through a series of well-executed troop movements early in the game.

Once England is out of the picture, spend some time building up your defenses and fortifying territories wherever possible. Remember, the Canadian terrain will still have a terrible defense rating even when you control it. Only when your

most vulnerable areas have been strengthened with reinforcements, and you've added significant numbers of fleets to your
navy, should you begin spending money on espionage and
subversion.

These efforts should be directed toward the remaining
neutral countries of South America that have ports. Since the
most vulnerable South American countries won't be adjacent
to any territories you control in the north, your navy will have
to lead the way. Once you get a foothold, continue to expand
your control with the ultimate goal of controlling the entire region. If you can achieve this before the other major countries
realize what's going on and gang up on you, the economic bonus you receive for control of the region can help fund the
military buildup that will win the game.

30
Lords of Conquest

Anyone can be a Napoleon or Alexander the Great in Lords of Conquest, *a strategy game in which territories are taken and held by skillful attacks and tenacious defense. Conquer the known world by raising armies and navies, and then flinging them against the enemy. Little diplomacy required here, just military action.*

Lords of Conquest is a *war* game. To win, you must seize all your opponents' land holdings through military aggression. There are no such things as tolerance or peaceful coexistence. The only alliances grow from a shared desire to crush a mutual enemy. At the end of the game, the map will have become one color, and every piece of gold, coal, and timber—every weapon, boat, or horse in the empire—will belong to the winner.

There are several things that make *Lords of Conquest* different from conventional war games. One difference is that, instead of displaying a map divided into hundreds of tiny squares, or hexes, this game is played on a map composed of many irregularly shaped territories. Each territory's inherent strength is based on the number of friendly territories bordering it, not its terrain type.

There are, in fact, only two kinds of terrain—land and water. Some territories, however, contain natural resources that can provide the controlling player with wealth or military strength. Careful management of these resources and wise spending of your empire's wealth are just as important as knowing where and when to build up your defenses or attack the enemy. To be proclaimed a Lord of Conquest, you must either capture all of the enemy's land, or, and more likely, you must acquire enough wealth and power to build three cities and successfully defend them for a year.

Territory Selection

After deciding on a map to battle over, players then take turns selecting individual territories. It's impossible to overemphasize the importance of these initial choices. Although a good selection of territories won't guarantee you a victory, it can certainly tilt the scales in your favor. A poor selection of territories, on the other hand, will almost certainly lead to defeat.

Resources

Since your goal is to build and defend three cities for a year, and cities can be acquired only with gold or other resources, you should try to select some territories that will start paying back in resources right away. Naturally, gold is an important commodity, but don't leave yourself without any pasture land. Not only do the horses that spring from pasture land add strength to the home territory, but in time, they can spread throughout your empire or even be brought by boat to islands. Also, horses' ability to join in on attacks up to two territories away, and transport weapons, makes them much more valuable than they might first appear.

Other resources such as timber, coal, and iron are also important, especially if you find yourself short of gold. For example, at the intermediate level and above, you can substitute one iron unit and one coal for two gold units, to buy a weapon. Similarly, instead of four gold, you can use only one gold with a coal, an iron, and a timber unit, to build a city. And don't forget the importance of timber when you're playing at levels where boat building is allowed.

Figure 30-1. Resources

GOLD PASTURE IRON COAL TIMBER HORSES SHIPS WEAPONS STOCK-PILE

Finally, although acquiring resources is essential to your winning the game, in some instances, picking a resource-containing territory during the initial selection phase isn't the best choice. For instance, if you select a gold-containing territory that is almost totally enclosed by your opponent's territories, you're bound to lose it the first time your opponent attacks.

Continuity

A territory's strength, both offensively and defensively, depends in large part on the number and strength of surrounding territories. Once all of the resource-containing territories have been selected, choose territories that border on those you already own. You can, thus, build an interlocking union that will hold up against enemy attack and allow you easily to expand.

Interference

Whenever possible, try to interfere with the opposition's plans. Obviously, other players will also hope to select resource-containing territories that are mutually supportive. Anytime you can jump in between two of the opponent's chosen territories while expanding your own domain, and possibly even snatching up a resource, do it. However, be careful when you use this divide-and-conquer approach because, as already mentioned, areas surrounded by enemy territory are usually the first to fall.

Guard Your Stockpile

After all players have selected their territories, you must place your stockpile in one that you own. Think of the stockpile as your Fort Knox. It represents the total accumulated wealth (gold and resources) that you've earned during the production phases. When an opponent captures the territory containing your stockpile, he or she gets all of your acquired wealth (but not the individual resources that produced the wealth). That can mark the beginning of the end for your empire; you'll be penniless during the next development phase, while your opponent uses the captured loot to strengthen territories and build cities.

Tuck your stockpile away in the safest possible corner of your empire. Peninsulas are a good bet, provided you control any bordering territories. However, often the safest territory for your stockpile will be right in the middle of the total area you control. During the shipment phases of each turn, you also have an opportunity to move your stockpile to a new location. Whenever you're selecting a location for your stockpile, keep in mind the number of consecutive attacks your opponent will be able to launch before you have a chance to respond. Often, a territory that looks like a perfectly safe home for your stockpile turns out to be quite vulnerable, once the enemy has taken over a couple of the bordering territories.

Development

The development phase is just as important as the conquest phase. The decisions you make here determine whether you can expand and defend your empire, or whether you must sit idly by while your opponent gobbles up your territories. With the wealth produced by your resource territories, you can purchase weapons, develop cities, or, at the advanced and expert levels, build boats during the development phase.

Placing Weapons

Just as important as being able to afford weapons, though, is knowing where to put them. Since a weapon adds just as much strength to adjacent territories as it does to its home territory, don't feel that you have to put weapons into territories that are directly threatened. By placing a weapon in a territory that's one territory removed from any enemy-controlled land, you can protect two or three territories simultaneously. A horse in the same territory adds to a weapon's usefulness by providing you with transportation to attacks as much as two territories away. Thus, by careful placement and shipment of your weapons, you'll be able to pose a threat along a wide front, even if your military budget is somewhat limited.

Cities

Buying cities won't immediately boost your military strength (at least to the extent that weapons do), but over the course of a couple of game turns, they can prove to be your most powerful assets. First, cities add two defensive strength points to their home and adjacent territories. Not bad considering that weapons only add three (see Table 30-1). Second, cities immediately double the production of all resources in the home and adjacent territories, letting you build even more cities and buy more weapons. This can often have a snowball effect—you can become so powerful so quickly, your opponent can be swallowed up without much of a fight.

The best place for a city is in a territory bordering as many friendly, resource-containing territories as possible. The worst place for a city is anywhere that the enemy will be able to capture it. Remember, once a city has been captured, there's usually little chance of winning it back.

Table 30-1. Defensive Force Points

	Home Territory	Adjacent Territory
Weapon	3	3
City[1]	2	2
Boat[2]	2	0
Horse[3]	1	1

[1] Cities double the production of resources in both their home territories and adjacent territories.

[2] Boats can transport horses and weapons into an attacked territory as long as there is a water route from the boat's home territory to the territory being attacked.

[3] Horses can transport weapons to attacks as much as two territories away.

Boats

Boats add as much defensive strength to their home territories as do cities. However, boats do nothing to improve the defensive or offensive strength of adjacent territories. On the attack, boats do nothing to improve your offensive strength unless you specifically bring them to the attack.

The one advantage that boats do possess over weapons and cities, however, is that two or more may be placed in a single territory. Weapons and cities, remember, may be distributed only one to a territory. This combination of strengths and weaknesses makes boats of little strategic value unless they are your only remaining option for adding defensive strength to a threatened territory, or unless you're planning an attack that requires boat transportation.

One final note about the development phase: Although weapons and boats can add strength to a territory, don't feel you always have to purchase something simply because you have the capability. The weapon or boat you pass up one turn can become a city the next. Unless you have a specific purpose in mind for a weapon or boat, save your money for a city. Even when your empire is crumbling around you, you may still be able to win by building enough cities that survive.

The Conquest

During the conquest phase of each turn, you're allowed two attacks against enemy-held territories. The player who attacks first, changes from year to year. Thus, in a two-player game, or in a solo contest against the computer, each player gets two conquests (four consecutive attacks) in a row before the other player can retaliate. Keep this in mind as you plan your offensive strategy.

For example, when you're attacking, don't simply look for a weaker enemy territory and pounce on it. Plan out an entire series of two or more attacks before assaulting a single territory. Take into account the added strength your transported horses and weapons will bring to the captured areas. Also, consider any enemy weapons or resources that you may capture along the way.

Perhaps the most important skill you can develop is the ability to quickly calculate a territory's strength in force points. One of the reasons the computer is such a formidable opponent is that it can almost instantly figure the strength of every territory on the map. By doing the same, you'll be able to spot weaknesses in the enemy's empire and can plan your attacks accordingly. Until you become proficient at calculating territorial strength, you can use the scouting report available through the conquest menu to get force counts. The report also provides information on individual territories and the contents of each player's stockpile. Remember, in a game of empire building like *Lords of Conquest,* information may be your most important resource.

★ APPENDICES ★

★ ★ ★ ★ ★ ★ ★ ★ ★

A
Alphabetical Listing of War Games

Ace	Spinnaker
Ace of Aces	Accolade
After Pearl	SuperWare
Air Rescue	MicroProse
Arcticfox	Electronic Arts
Auto Duel	Origin Systems
Baltic 1985	Strategic Simulations
Battalion Commander	Strategic Simulations
Battle Command	Applied Computer Consultants
Battlecruiser	Strategic Simulations
Battle for Normandy	Strategic Simulations
Battlefront	Strategic Studies Group
Battlegroup	Strategic Simulations
Battle of Antietam	Strategic Simulations
Battle of Chickamauga	Game Designers' Workshop
Battle of the Atlantic	Simulations Canada
Battles in Normandy	Strategic Studies Group
Beach Head I and *II*	Access Software
Blue Powder Grey Smoke	Garde
B1 Nuclear Bomber	Avalon Hill
Breakthrough in the Ardennes	Strategic Simulations
Broadsides	Strategic Simulations
Carrier Force	Strategic Simulations
Carriers at War	Strategic Studies Group
Clear for Action	Avalon Hill
Colonial Conquest	Strategic Simulations
Combat Leader	Strategic Simulations
Commando	Data East
Computer Ambush	Strategic Simulations
Computer Bismarck	Strategic Simulations
Computer Diplomacy	Avalon Hill
Conflict in Vietnam	MicroProse
Crusade in Europe	MicroProse

Dam Busters	Accolade
Decision in the Desert	MicroProse
Destroyer	Epyx
Destroyer Escort	MicroProse
Dnieper River Line	Avalon Hill
Dreadnoughts	Avalon Hill
Eagles	Strategic Simulations
Europe Ablaze	Strategic Studies Group
F-15 Strike Eagle	MicroProse
Fall Gelb	Simulations Canada
Field of Fire	Strategic Simulations
Fifth Eskadra	Simulations Canada
50 Mission Crush	Strategic Simulations
Fighter Command	Strategic Simulations
Gato	Spectrum Holobyte
Geopolitique 1990	Strategic Simulations
Germany 1985	Strategic Simulations
Gettysburg: The Turning Point	Strategic Simulations
Golan Front	Simulations Canada
Grey Seas, Grey Skies	Simulations Canada
Guadal Canal Campaign	Strategic Simulations
Guderian	Avalon Hill
Gulf Strike	Avalon Hill
Gunship	MicroProse
Hellcat Ace	MicroProse
High Roller	Mindscape
Infiltrator	Mindscape
Iwo Jima—1945/Falklands—1982	Firebird
Jet	Sublogic
Jet Combat Simulator	Epyx
Kampfgruppe	Strategic Simulations
Knights of the Desert	Strategic Simulations
Kursk Campaign	Simulations Canada
Legionnaire	Avalon Hill
Lords of Conquest	Electronic Arts
Mech Brigade	Strategic Simulations
MiG Alley Ace	MicroProse
Nam	Strategic Simulations
Napoleon at Waterloo	Krentek Software
NATO Commander	MicroProse
North Atlantic '86	Strategic Simulations
Norway 1985	Strategic Simulations

Objective: Kursk	Strategic Simulations
Ogre	Origin Systems
Operation Market Garden	Strategic Simulations
Operation Overlord	Simulations Canada
Operation Whirlwind	Brøderbund
Panzer Grenadier	Strategic Simulations
Panzer Jagd	Avalon Hill
Panzers East	Avalon Hill
RDF 1985	Strategic Simulations
Reforger '88	Strategic Simulations
Road to Moscow	Game Designers' Workshop
Rome and the Barbarians	Krentek
Rommel at Gazala	Simulations Canada
Rommel: Battles for Tobruk	Game Designers' Workshop
Russia: The Great War in the East 1941–1945	Strategic Studies Group
Seventh Fleet	Simulations Canada
Sieg in Afrika	Simulations Canada
Silent Service	MicroProse
Skyfox	Electronic Arts
Sonar Search	Signal Computer Consultants
Spitfire Ace	MicroProse
Spitfire 40	Avalon Hill
Stalingrad Campaign	Simulations Canada
Super Huey I and *II*	Cosmi
Tac	Avalon Hill
Tanktics	Avalon Hill
Theatre Europe	DataSoft
Thunderchopper	ActionSoft
Tigers in the Snow	Strategic Simulations
Top Gunner Collection	MicroProse
Under Fire	Avalon Hill
Up Periscope!	ActionSoft
U.S.A.A.F.	Strategic Simulations
Wargame Construction Set	Strategic Simulations
War in Russia	Strategic Simulations
War in the South Pacific	Strategic Simulations
Warship	Strategic Simulations
Wings of War	Strategic Simulations

B
War Game Manufacturers

Actionsoft
122-4 S. Race St.
Urbana, IL 61801

The Avalon Hill Game Company
4517 Harford Rd.
Baltimore, MD 21214

Brøderbund
17 Paul Dr.
San Rafael, CA 94903

Electronic Arts
1820 Gateway Dr.
San Mateo, CA 94404

Epyx
1043 Kiel Ct.
Sunnyvale, CA 94809

MicroProse Simulation Software
120 Lakefront Dr.
Hunt Valley, MD 21030

Mindscape
3444 Dundee Rd.
Northbrook, IL 60062

Origin Systems
340 Harvey Rd.
Manchester, NH 03103

Strategic Simulations
1046 N. Rengstorff Ave.
Mountain View, CA 94043

Strategic Studies Group
1747 Orleans Ct.
Walnut Creek, CA 94598

subLOGIC
713 Edgebrook Dr.
Champaign, IL 61820